Squash

Ken Weatherley and Ian Robinson

Macdonald Guidelines

Editorial manager
Chester Fisher
Series editor
Jim Miles
Editor
Neil Tennant
Designer
Peter Benoist
Picture researcher
Jenny Golden
Production
Penny Kitchenham

Made and printed by
Waterlow (Dunstable) Ltd

ISBN 0 356 06438 7
(cased edition)
ISBN 0 356 06038 1
(paperback edition)

Contents

© Macdonald Educational Ltd 1979
First published 1979
Macdonald Educational Ltd,
Holywell House, Worship Street,
London EC2A 2EN

The story of squash

Squash, or more properly, squash rackets, is one of today's most popular sports. There are probably more than one and a half million players of both sexes in Britain alone, and the Squash Rackets Association estimates that half of these are regular players. New courts and centres continue to be built and, although the rate of increase is declining, the squash boom is still very much with us.

But it has not always been so. In fact for years squash, like its relative, rackets, was primarily the game of the upper classes. But a tremendous surge of interest, beginning in the 1960s, has made squash a game of the people.

Racket sports

To discover the origins of the game, it is necessary to go back at least 150 years. However, some historians insist that squash is the result of a development of the racket sports which began as long ago as the 13th century.

The ancient 'jeu de paume', in which a sheepskin ball was struck with the palm of the hand, is the most convenient starting point. This game, originating in France and Italy, was played in Britain around 1275, and the version which was played inside buildings (usually in the courtyard) was the one which gave us the first recognizable modern term: the court.

Royal patronage

It took a further three centuries for the first racket to appear and by this time the game had achieved a measure of respectability. The Tudor kings and queens found the game so enjoyable that they had courts built at Hampton Court, Windsor and Whitehall, and their patronage of the game caused it to become known as 'royal tennis'. (The origin of the term 'tennis' is obscure, but the most likely theory is that the French called *'tenez!'*—'take this!'—before serving.)

Those who have seen royal or 'real' tennis played will not find it difficult to understand the transition from that game to the more modern lawn tennis. The change from real tennis to rackets is more difficult to follow, although it is generally accepted that tennis fathered rackets.

Rackets was first played in Fleet debtors prison (near Fleet Street) and the game was established by the early 19th century. Dickens describes a court in his *Pickwick Papers* (1836–7), and the first 'world champion' was one Robert Mackey, an inmate of the Fleet.

▲ The French played *jeu de paume*— 'game of the hand'—over seven centuries ago. All of today's racket sports are descended from this game.

It might well be assumed that a game played in the taverns and public houses, as well as in prison, was not likely to be accepted by the more respectable classes. Inexplicably, however, the game was played in Harrow School in 1822 and soon afterwards at Eton and Winchester. For the first time, also, the court became enclosed within four walls.

Rackets flourished during the latter part of the 19th century, and was exported by the armed forces to Canada, America, India and the Argentine. The Queen's Club was built in West London and became what it is today, the headquarters of rackets. However, the success of rackets was shortlived. After World War I the cost of building the courts (which are approximately twice the size of the modern squash court with walls and floors of cement) became prohibitive.

The rise of squash coincided with the demise of rackets, and now the only rackets courts which remain (about 20) are to be found in the public schools and in long established clubs like Queen's. Nevertheless, it is an extremely interesting and demanding game. The hard ball reaches speeds in excess of 100 mph, calling for a quick eye, and the angles created by the use of the side and rear walls, with the additional hazard of spin, put sound judgement and nimble footwork at a premium.

The origins of squash

It may be of some consolation to those who are already squash players to know that the problem of court time is not a new one. Indeed, it is at the root of the game. For when rackets was so popular that the schoolboys of Harrow could not get on to the court, they improvised with an india rubber ball, using any walls they could find. This was almost certainly how squash originated, probably in the mid-19th century.

Gradually slower balls were used, the slowest being a punctured variety known as 'the holer'. But squash was really only regarded as a training aid to rackets. Later, when rackets was declining and in order to protect the game, many purists dispensed with squash, arguing that the modern game would be the death of rackets.

After 1918, the game of squash became formalized with the introduction of firm rules, including the definitive court dimensions and the establishment of a governing body. And not before time. The armed forces had again taken the game abroad, this time to the new lands of Australia and South Africa. The Americans and Canadians had formalized rules in 1907 and 1911.

Unfortunately, the game on the other side of the Atlantic has developed in a different way. A harder ball is used in a larger court and with a different method of scoring. Had the rules in Britain been drawn up earlier, it is possible that this hardball version would not exist today. As it is, the softball or international game is now played in over 40 countries all over the world.

An indoor game

Although squash superseded rackets, it remained in the shadow of lawn tennis until the early 1960s. That squash should

▲ Rackets at Harrow School. This illustration clearly shows how only two walls and a courtyard were necessary to play the early version of the game.

have outstripped its more glamorous counterpart as a participatory sport is due to a number of factors.

Unlike tennis, squash is a game which is relatively easy to learn. In tennis, the net is a physical obstacle which the ball must clear, but the player must also get over the technical difficulty of bringing the ball down within the confines of the court. There being no net in squash (only a small 'board'), the player has only the out-of-court lines to contend with, and the rallies are not constantly cut short. So long as a player is not in extreme difficulties, he should be able to keep the ball in play.

The other major difference is in the rackets used in the two games. While a tennis racket weighs about 375g (13oz), a squash racket averages a little less than than 200g (8oz). It is thus more easy to wield, particularly for women.

The lack of tennis facilities which exist in some parts of the world, especially the type of courts on which many world class tournaments are played, and particularly the shortage of indoor facilities, are two reasons why squash has benefited at the expense of tennis. The vagaries of the weather do not interfere with the arrangements made by squash players, although, as we shall see, they might affect the kind of game that is played. Furthermore, because squash is an indoor game, it can be played at any time of the day or night.

Club squash

There is another area where squash has organized itself more efficiently than tennis. While it is rarely an accepted principle in club tennis that a member can book a specific time for his game *and* choose his opponent, (although this has to be the case where there is a shortage of public and covered courts), a squash player can appear minutes before his reserved court time and be sure of his session being uninterrupted.

It is perhaps worthwhile noting here that because it is an accepted principle in squash that a player hires the court for a specific period, the club or centre letting the court is to some degree ensuring the continued well-being of its facilities and the popularity of the game. Squash clubs, for the most part, are new and reasonably well appointed. Tennis clubs, on the other hand, are more often than not relics of a bygone age: wooden-built, cold and uncomfortable, because they lack the additional

▶ A game of real tennis in progress at Queen's Club, London.

funds created by court hire to use for renovations.

Finance is at the heart of another reason for the growth of squash. In only a few cases will tennis clubs be run on a proprietary basis, while it is reasonably common in squash. Businessmen have taken the opportunity of a good return on money invested. Of course, tennis has an inherent disadvantage in this respect in that a tennis court is approximately six times the size of a squash court. The cost of a site is proportionately greater.

The pressures of modern living mean that it is sometimes impossible to spend as much time as one would like in playing sport. But with the dynamic nature and the structure of squash, it is possible to play for half an hour during a lunch break or after work. Given that the player is matched against an opponent of similar ability, the half-hour can be quite exhausting for a newcomer to the game. An old hand might not be played out, but at least he will feel that he has worked hard. This feeling may not be achieved after a round of golf or after an hour's tennis. More and more working people are taking up squash because it's both quick and convenient, and it is a good way to keep fit. Most people appreciate the need for physical exercise, and squash is a method which is neither boring, because it is competitive, nor too time-consuming.

The Barrington phenomenon

Perhaps what has caught the imagination of the public more than any other single factor in squash was the emergence of a great world champion. Jonah Barrington rose from obscurity during the course of two seasons to win both the Amateur Championship and the Open Championship in the same year, 1966. While this may not seem as difficult to achieve as the Grand

▲ The young Jonah Barrington who became only the second man to win both the Open and the Amateur Championships in the same season.

▶ Barrington's many battles with Geoff Hunt have been a feature of his career.

Slam in tennis or golf (which comprise four championships) it had nevertheless been achieved only once before, by the legendary Amr of Egypt in 1932. It has not been achieved since, except again by Barrington. Now that most of the world's leading players are professional, a change largely wrought by Barrington, his record is likely to remain unbroken.

Barrington repeated the feat in 1967 and after turning professional, continued to be the dominant force in world squash for some years. His example raised the quality of competitive squash and although superior fitness was one of his principle assets, it would be idle to suggest that it was this alone which made him a cut above the rest.

All these factors contributed to the boom in squash which started around 1963 and which is still continuing. Then, there were 100,000 players compared with one and a half million now. During the period 1972–4 the number of courts was being increased at a rate of 20 per cent per annum; a remarkable expansion.

The future

For all that there are some factors which could limit the success of the game. For instance, how many of those one and a half million players have ever seen a top-class match live? The answer is probably less than one per cent. The SRA's championship court at Wembley caters for a few hundred spectators only. The advent of the glass back wall has increased the numbers who can watch, but inevitably there is a limit to the numbers who are able to see clearly.

One method of bringing squash to a larger audience could be television, but as yet no company has applied itself successfully to the problems of televising squash. The ball moves too quickly for a close-up camera to follow, and the long range camera has difficulty picking up the small ball. The disinterested observer is hardly likely to be encouraged to take up the game if he cannot see what is happening, and the committed player is frustrated because he is unable to appreciate the finer points.

Until these problems are solved, the top squash players are unlikely to be elevated to superstar status. But perhaps that is all to the good. Squash is, above all, a game to be played.

On the court

It has already been mentioned that the squash court is enclosed by four walls. Most traditional courts, out of necessity and convenience, also have a roof, giving the impression of a rectangular box. But the roof is not an integral part of the court. Indeed it can, and does, get in the way if it is built too low. So the roof of a championship court is set at a height which cannot conceivably interfere with play.

Until recently all the walls inside the box were made of a special plaster. However, in order to allow more people to see a game in progress, a special kind of glass was developed. At first the whole of the back wall was encased by the brickwork of the surrounding walls. This still meant that only people directly behind the court could see clearly, and that tiers of seats for spectators were impossible.

The first free-standing glass back wall was built at the Abbeydale Squash Club in Sheffield and the British Open was immediately moved there. Glass back walls are now an increasing feature of modern squash centres. Experiments are now being made with glass side walls too and there are indications that it will not be too long before the first court with three glass walls is in use.

The court floor is made of strips of hard wood, usually Canadian maple, although beech is sometimes used. These strips are laid on battens to give flexibility.

The final feature of the court, apart from the play lines, is the 'tin' or 'board'. This is situated on the front wall and is all that remains of the net used in the other racket sports from which squash evolved. A thin strip of wood runs along the front wall 50cm (19in) from the floor and this marks

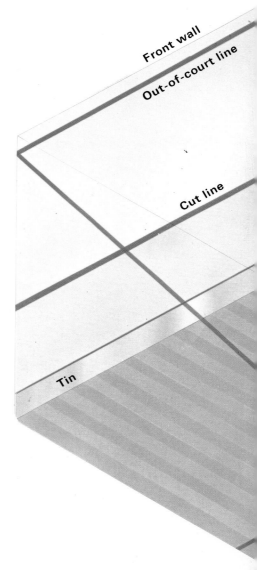

▲ A view of the squash court which may become commonplace as experiments with glass bring us nearer to the all-glass court. Greater spectator facilities could extend the popularity of the game.

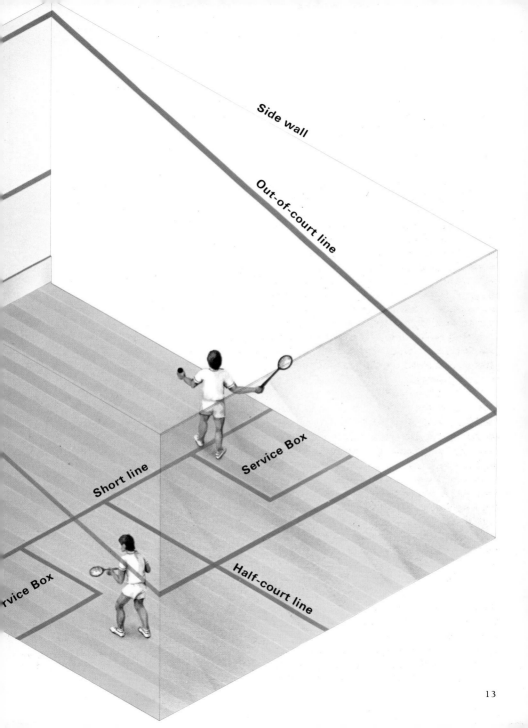

Side wall

Out-of-court line

Service Box

Short line

Service Box

Half-court line

the lower limit of the playing area on the front wall. Beneath the board is the tin which reaches to the floor. The different sounds made by the ball striking these surfaces are an aural aid in determining whether or not the ball was 'down' or out of play.

There are two other lines on the front wall. One, at a height of 1·8 metres (6ft) from the floor is the 'cut' line. Every service must strike the front wall above this line. The other, at a height of 4·5 metres (15ft) above the floor, is the upper limit of the playing area, and is called the 'out-of-court' line.

This upper out-of-court line continues along the other walls. On the back wall it is drawn horizontally at a height of 2 metres (7ft), and the side wall lines are drawn by joining the front and back wall out-of-court lines.

The remaining lines on the court are to be found on the floor. The 'short' line and the 'half-court' line are drawn to mark the area where the server must land his service. Within each of the quarters made by these lines there is a square called the service box, which specifies the position from which the service shall be delivered. The short line and half-court lines make a 'T'. This T is a critical landmark for all squash players.

The doubles court

It is possible to play doubles in squash, but to do so in a singles court can be a little dangerous. The rules prescribe a court 4 metres (13ft) longer and 1·2 metres (4ft) wider. The out-of-court line on the front wall is redrawn at twenty feet. Because of these basic alterations, all the other lines on the court must be drawn differently, and few courts exist. Squash has become overwhelmingly a singles game.

Rackets

A squash racket is, more or less, the same length as a tennis racket, but the head and frame are smaller, making it much lighter and more manageable than a tennis racket.

The dimensions of a tennis racket are nowhere defined, and although there have been many experiments with the shape and size of the head, the length does not vary more than 1cm ($\frac{1}{2}$in). In theory, if the right material could be found, a giant-sized racket with the aerodynamic properties of a conventional racket could be used.

This is not the case in squash, where the limitations are strictly imposed, primarily for the safety of the combatants. The racket

▶ There are plenty of manufacturers of squash rackets, clothing and accessories from which to choose. Clubs tend to prefer white clothes, but, apart from colour, absorbtion is a key factor.

must be no more than 67cm (27in) long nor more than 210cm (8½in) wide. There are further restrictions on the size of the head and the amount of wood used to make it. The head must be of wood and no other material, although the shaft and handle can be made of virtually anything.

There are a great number of rackets on the market from which to choose. They don't vary enormously in weight, grip, size and balance, although accomplished players will be able to discern from the feel of a racket whether one is lighter in the head than another. But there *will* be a large variation in price, and this can be due to the nature of the construction or the materials used. Flexibility and strength can be created at the same time through laminating several layers of wood. Bamboo is common in flexible rackets and beech in rigid ones. Price can also be a reflection of the cost of the raw materials employed in the racket. The beginner should settle for a cheap or medium-priced model, because in the early days, it is quite probable that a slight misjudgement near the walls will cause a costly breakage.

For the same reason it is advisable to begin with a synthetic, man-made string in the racket, as opposed to the more expensive natural gut string. Although the more advanced player gets more feel from gut, it is more likely to break and will not offer the beginner any great advantage.

It is important when choosing a racket to find one which feels comfortable in terms of weight, balance and grip. There are basically two types of grip: leather and towelling. Many players find that leather grips become slippery after a time, although this can be countered by roughening the leather or by the use of resin. Towelling grips absorb perspiration, but have a limited life. Unfortunately, squash being the energetic game that it is, it may be necessary to change towelling grips quite frequently.

Clothing

Towelling is sometimes used in squash clothing for the same reasons, but any

▼ Choice of racket is entirely personal, but you should protect your feet with thick socks and shoes designed for squash.

absorbent material will suffice. Again, comfort should be the watchword when choosing what to wear. There are no restrictions on design, but in most places white is the required colour.

Many players find that wristlets or sweatbands are useful accessories. They stop perspiration running into the racket hand and can also be used for mopping the brow. Headbands are also popular for this and can stop perspiration dropping on the lenses of players' spectacles.

Without doubt the most important items of the squash player's outfit are his socks and shoes. Constant twisting and turning can easily cause blisters and a good thick pair of socks will provide the first line of defence. Some players find that two pairs of socks are more comfortable, but if your shoes are a good fit, one should suffice.

Shoes will need to be light but supple. There are several brands of shoe made exclusively for squash. While these custom-built varieties are preferable, any white shoe is acceptable unless it has a black sole, which marks the floor.

The ball

The dimensions of the squash ball are, again, strictly defined. It is made of a rubber and butyl composition and it is extremely soft. Although it is not at all bouncy when it is cold, the constant battering it receives from rackets and walls warms the air inside and makes the ball more lively.

There are four different kinds of ball and they are marked with a coloured dot to denote the variation in bounce. The slowest is yellow, and white, red and blue are progressively faster. Beginners should start with blue, which will give them more time to make their shots because it bounces higher and longer than the others.

▼ Four speeds of squash ball are available: blue, red, white and yellow. The fastest, the blue spot, should be used by beginners because it will give them more time to play their strokes. The slowest, yellow, seems dead by comparison until it is warmed up.

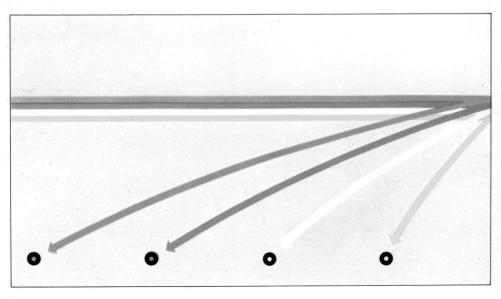

Modern squash

The Squash Rackets Association (SRA) is the central authority in Britain for the administration of the men's game. The SRA's sphere of operations, sometimes delegated to the county associations, includes the organization and playing of the game, the rules, championships, international matches and tours, and the resolution of disputes arising from any of these areas. Virtually every club in the land, whether or not it has courts of its own is affiliated to the SRA, and pays an affiliation fee. Thus over 1200 clubs come under the jurisdiction of the SRA. Schools and colleges affiliate in the same way.

The fees from these clubs account for 20 per cent of the SRA's income. A further 4 per cent comes from the fees paid by individual members of the association. Individual membership gives spectators the opportunity to book seats in advance at SRA-run events and players the chance to

▼ The Championship court at Wembley Squash centre, owned by the SRA. All the instructional photographs were taken here with Gawain Briars (1977 British Junior Champion) and co-author Ian Robinson.

play at many affiliated clubs under the 'visiting membership' conditions. It also bestows the right to attend SRA Annual General Meetings.

By far the largest items of income come from the Sports Council, who supply 31 per cent of the total, and from sponsorship and donations which account for a further 30 per cent. The remaining 15 per cent is accounted for by the sale of publications and from fees earned by the technical services department, and the profits from the championship court at Wembley, which the SRA owns.

On the other side of the balance sheet, the SRA spends money on coaching, tournaments and tours, as it is responsible for the selection of representative teams and for championship events. It also produces a big, informative handbook. Research and development is an important item of expenditure, and finally, of course, there are the considerable costs of administering an already large and growing sport.

Ten per cent of the affiliation fees are returned direct to the county associations and 35 per cent goes to the Women's Squash Rackets Association (WSRA). The WSRA evolved from a ladies' committee originally set up by the SRA in 1932 to organise international events for women. It became an association in its own right in 1934. The WSRA controls the women's game in the same way that the SRA controls the men's, and as such is responsible for 35 per cent of the squash players in this country at the present time.

Coaching

Both associations put a great deal of store in coaching and this is obviously for the long-term benefit of the game. The more players are encouraged to play, the healthier the game becomes and the more potential champions emerge. This is why much of the coaching work is done at grass roots level. Although the coaching standards are decided by each association, there is a measure of uniformity. There are two kinds of coach: under the SRA the first is one who holds the elementary coaching certificate, which means that he or she is competent to teach beginners and more advanced players either as individuals or in groups; and the second is one who holds the advanced coaching certificate, and he will be able to advise the players of good standard.

Apart from a great many elementary and advanced coaches who are amateurs, there are also professionals who will very likely be members of the Squash Rackets Professional's Association (SRPA). Members of this association include touring professionals and coaches who earn part or all of their living from the game.

The international scene

The SRA is itself a member of two other organisations; the European Squash Rackets Federation (ESRF) and the International Squash Rackets Federation (ISRF). The ESRF was set up in 1973, runs a European Championship and is concerned for the welfare of the game in Europe. Rapid progress is being made in what used to be a barren area for squash and there are already some promising players, particularly from Sweden, and some very modern facilities. Most activity centres around France, Germany, Benelux and Scandinavia, with Germany's rate of growth suggesting that it might be a major force in a few year's time.

▶ Heather McKay (Blundell) who, together with Janet Shardlow (Morgan), has dominated women's squash since the war.

The ISRF is the world governing body, a role it took over from the SRA, which had been the *de facto* governing body since 1929. The ISRF was founded in 1966 and one of its first acts was to set up an official World Amateur Championship to replace the British Amateur which had hitherto been regarded as the world championship. The ISRF decides disputes of all kinds, but perhaps its most important function is to decide on changes and amendments to the rules.

Competitions

Competition is at the heart of squash. Almost every club runs a ladder or a league competition, or both, in which every member of the club is entitled to participate. The ladder is a kind of ranking list, with the best players at the top and the worst at the bottom. The rules vary from place to place, but the basis of the ladder competition is that any player can challenge someone above him on the list (usually restricted to a maximum number of places). If the challenger wins, he occupies the place of the beaten player, and all the intervening players are moved down one place to accommodate him.

In the leagues, players are again categorized according to form, but in this competition all the players play each other either once or twice. Allocation of points again varies. In some cases you may simply score two points for a win; in others you may score a point for every game you win. In the end the league relegates and promotes players to different leagues. Both the ladder and the leagues usually operate throughout the season, although depending on the size, the leagues could be completed twice a season.

Just for variety there is generally the club knockout once a year. Here there are usually eight seeded players and the rest are drawn by lot. There is always the chance, therefore, that you could be drawn against the club champion, an opportunity which might not come your way very often.

The club champion, apart from being involved on the ladder and in the leagues probably represents the club in another league. Most clubs field at least one team in the local league, which gives competition for the best players in an area. There are hundreds of leagues in operation throughout the country, and even the most modest player may reasonably aspire to play in these leagues, even if it is in a lowly division.

If your club champion plays in Division 1 of a county league, he will in all probability be verging on county class. Many counties run an individual ladder of their best players in order to establish a ranking list which will help the selectors. A player of this calibre could also take part in any of the small weekend tournaments which are run up and down the country. Indeed, these tournaments are open to any club player and your game can only improve by playing against players of a higher standard. Even if you do lose easily at first, you can learn a lot by watching and the atmosphere is normally congenial.

The very best county players play in a different circuit of tournaments, some of them restricted to just 16 players. These are the very best amateur players in the country. From time to time there may even be some foreign opposition, especially around the time of the British Amateur and perhaps the British Open.

The most important tournament for amateur players is the World Amateur Championships. The British Amateur, which had been regarded until 1966 as the world title, ranks next in importance. For different reasons the World Team Championships is highly regarded, as is the

▶ Jonathan Leslie, a barrister-at-law who is one of Britain's top amateur players, in a match against Gogi Alauddin, former Amateur Champion and one of the first squash professionals.

British Amateur Closed, although it is restricted to British players.

The standard of competition at this type of tournament has reached a very high level indeed. Already some of the top amateur players are beginning to trouble some of the highly ranked professionals. Some of these so-called amateurs are devoting almost all of their time and energy to improving their squash. Players like Jonathan

Leslie, who combines the duties of barrister at law and British No. 1, could become a rarity in top amateur squash in the not too distant future.

Amateur status

The problem for amateur players who want to play on a full-time basis is obviously how to finance themselves while they play. But it is not as difficult as it may seem to the layman, because in many cases the rules relating to amateur status as laid down by the SRA allow expenses to be paid to players. In others the rules have been relaxed to a point where there is little difference between an amateur and a professional.

The rules state that a player cannot retain amateur status if he derives any financial gain from the game, except that he is allowed to be remunerated for any coaching work that he undertakes which is approved by the SRA, for any writing about the game, and for selling equipment relating to the game. However, he may not advertise equipment.

There would seem to be no leeway for payments to players at first sight. But 'no financial gain' does not exclude recompense for expenses incurred in travelling, and for hotels and meals, and while in some circumstances this may not amount to more than a few pounds, in others it could mean that a player is living quite comfortably. While those expenses are genuinely incurred by a player, he remains strictly within the law. He is making no actual gain.

But squash has reached the same impasse that tennis reached in the sixties. Tournaments profited by using cheap labour (the amateur player) while charging the consumer (the spectator) top rates for the product. Not unreasonably, the players demanded payment for their services and devised ways of circumventing the rules. A player is not in breach of the rules if he accepts a wager of £200 offered by the tournament organisation for drinking a glass of orange juice. Neither is he if he accepts a similar wager from a sports goods manufacturer. But to all intents and purposes the player is receiving a fee for appearing at the tournament, and a payment for using a particular piece of equipment and indirectly advertising it.

The disadvantage with such a system is that everything remains secret and somehow underhand. Worse, a player who plays a stormer and beats the No. 1 seed is not rewarded for his efforts while the seeded player reclines in luxury at the hotel. Worse still is the possibility that the match was fixed.

Open events

Tennis went open in 1968 and apart from players from some of the Communist bloc and a few very young players from America intent on succeeding in the national collegiate championships, which retain a great

► Lars Kvant of Sweden, one of the stars of an emergent squash nation.

deal of importance, there are no amateur players in the first 500 tennis players in the world. What amateur events remain pay no expenses and no prize money.

Competition between amateur and professional squash players has always been possible in open events. The WSRA have already taken the initiative, declaring the game open in September 1978, and although talks continue, it remains to be seen whether or not the men's game will follow.

Professional competition

The professional tour has not operated for long, but the momentum is quickening and the number of players who play competitively for most of the time is on the increase. The best professionals can reasonably expect to earn in excess of £20,000 from prize money and endorsements. Since all their expenses can be paid by tournament organisers, the top players can earn a fair living. Prize money levels are rising rapidly and, so long as the spectators can be accommodated in larger numbers, should continue to increase.

Prize money comes from sponsorship by major companies. Sports goods companies tend to restrict themselves to smaller events and to securing the endorsements of the top players for their products. They also give away their products to help promising players. The major sponsors in Britain over the last few years have included Lucas and Avis (British Open), Pakistan International Airlines (PIA World Series), Sun Life (British Amateur) and Langham Life (Women's British Open and Home Internationals).

These companies have been persuaded to spend their money in squash because the potential market is large. Due to the increase in the number of players, more and more sponsors find squash an attractive sponsorship proposition. The result has been a proliferation of tournaments, exhibitions, challenge matches and other competitions during the last few years.

While the major companies take care of the international type of tournament, smaller and sometimes local firms provide for more modest ventures. Very often the best way for a small club to see the professionals in the flesh is to put on an exhibition. Whilst this is not the same as a serious competitive match, the professionals are aware that it is their duty to promote the game they earn their living from, and can usually be relied upon to put on an excellent evening's entertainment. Indeed when the professional tour was in its infancy, many professionals relied upon this kind of arrangement for their livelihood.

But their sights will be firmly set on one of the major honours in the professional game. The first amongst them is the World Open. Rather like the relationship between the World Amateur and the British Amateur, the British Open, for so long the unofficial world championship, is second, and behind that there are the Opens of Australia and South Africa.

◀ Mike Grundy, a member of the Championship-winning Yorkshire team.

How to play

Because squash is a game of explosive movement, it is often impossible for a beginner to analyze a stroke made by an accomplished player with a view to improving his own technique. Ideally a slow-motion camera trained on a world-class player would best demonstrate good stroke production. Having no such aid, the best thing to do is to study strokes in isolation and add movement later.

The object of the game

The game begins with the service, which must be delivered from either of the two service boxes in the rear quarters of the court. The server is known as 'hand in' and the receiver is 'hand out'. In order not to be penalized for a foot fault, the server must have the whole of one foot entirely within the service box.

The object of the service is to hit the ball onto the front wall above the cut line so that it falls within the opposite rear quarter of the court. The server may make use of the side and rear walls when serving, but the ball must hit the front wall first. He is also allowed one fault. In this case the receiver may elect to volley the ball before it has bounced—even though the ball might have landed outside the correct quarter if the receiver had allowed the ball to bounce—or play the ball even though it has been judged a fault.

The receiver must strike the ball so that it again hits the front wall and rebounds into play. Again he may make use of the side and rear walls in order to make good his return. The players then play the ball alternately. A player wins a rally if his opponent cannot do any of the following.

1 Return the ball to the front wall before the ball has bounced twice on the floor.

2 Keep the ball within the out-of-court boundaries (in other words if the ball hits any wall above the out-of-court line or below the board).

3 Avoid being struck by the ball (and this includes his clothing and his racket) except where a 'let' can be awarded (see below p. 66).

A player also wins a rally if his opponent strikes the ball twice consecutively.

Scoring

Although a player may win a rally in one of the ways discussed above, it does not necessarily mean that he has scored a point. For in squash only the server may score. If the server has won the rally, he continues serving from alternate service boxes until the receiver wins the rally.

The receiver then becomes 'hand in' and the server 'hand out'.

Winning

A game in squash is won by the player who reaches nine points first, provided he has a margin of two points over his opponent. In the event of the score reaching eight points all, the receiver has the option of calling 'no set' or 'set two'. In the first case the game is won by the player who scores the next point; and in the second by the player who first reaches ten points, regardless of the margin. A game can therefore be scored 9—8, 10—8, or 10—9. A match is usually the best of five games, so the first to win three games is the winner.

Doubles

In doubles the rules are quite different. Any side winning

▶ Playing the ball just before its second bounce.

a rally scores a point and the game is scored to 15 instead of nine. Each team plays alternately and either member of each team may play the ball at any time. Because of the lack of courts, doubles is played mostly on a singles court, and in the confined space injuries can occur. If you do attempt the doubles version, remember to occupy the space around the T when you are not striking the ball. There you will be in less danger and the game will be considerably more enjoyable.

Lets

Finally, there is one method of scoring points which has not yet been mentioned. It is the reasonably complex rule relating to lets and penalty points and this is dealt with in a later chapter (see p. 66).

The grip

Before discussing the basic forehand and backhand drives and how these are modified to produce the drop shot, the lob and the volley, it is essential to ensure that the grip we intend to use for these strokes is sound.

(Note: all instructions will be for right-handers. Left-handers should do the reverse.)

Holding the racket by the shaft in the left hand so that the face of the racket is invisible, 'shake hands' with the handle. If you are gripping the racket correctly you will have formed a 'V' on top of the handle with the line of your thumb and forefinger.

The grip

▼ The orthodox grip should make a 'V' between the thumb and forefinger on top of the handle with the fingers spread comfortably. Grip the racket firmly, but not too tightly.

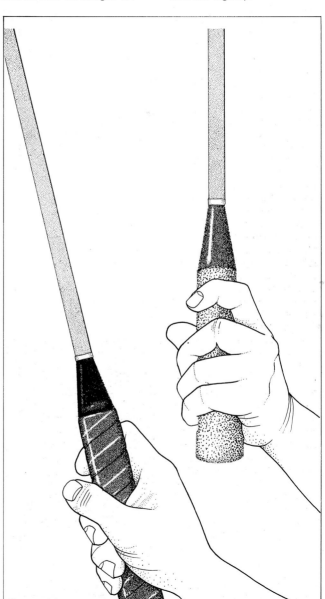

Ideally this 'V' will be a little to the left of centre. Any small adjustment to this is not disastrous but large variations may create great difficulties later on and will almost certainly lead to unorthodox stroke-making. The orthodox grip will allow you to play every stroke in the game.

Be careful not to make a fist of your hand with the racket locked within. Spread the fingers a comfortable distance apart as this will help to give you a better feel later on.

Feel and control are what we are aiming for first and they will not be achieved if the racket is held tightly all the time. The arm and wrist will tire quickly so grip the racket firmly. Gradually it will become second nature to relax the grip slightly when you are not actually striking the ball.

There is a ridge at the end of the handle of most rackets and this is to prevent the racket slipping from your grasp. It is called the butt, and in the orthodox grip it will not come into contact with the fleshy part of the hand. Some players prefer to have the butt in the palm of their hands but, although this will undoubtedly lend more power to their strokes, it will be at the expense of control.

Cocking the wrist

The next basic to understand and master is the cocking of the wrist. If you extend your arm so that it is parallel with the ground, your racket will make an angle of 90° with your arm when the wrist is cocked. If you drop your wrist, the racket will become almost a continuation of your arm, parallel to the ground. It is essential that the wrist is cocked when gripping the racket because the wrist must be in this position at the beginning of every stroke. Not only that, it will remain cocked throughout every stroke. Of course, there will be times when this will not be possible because an opponent has made life so difficult that improvization is necessary. But for the basic strokes, the wrist must remain cocked.

Stroke production

Imagine you are standing in the middle of a squash court, on the 'T', facing the front wall. Any ball which comes to your right will be a forehand and any to your left a

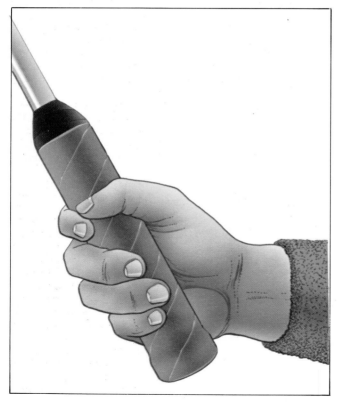

◀ The head of the racket should always be above the wrist. This allows the wrist to contribute more power to the stroke by rotating from side to side.

▶ The arc of the swing.

backhand. In order to play either of the shots you will need to turn the body and the feet so that you are sideways on to the front wall. From this position you will be able to play almost all the shots you will need.

There are four factors that will make the stroke powerful. The first is obviously the speed with which the arm brings the racket to meet the ball. Clearly, the further the arm moves, the easier it is to hit the ball harder.

But the second is equally important and it relies on cocking the wrist. Repeat the exercise to ensure that the wrist is cocked. Now, without letting your wrist drop, turn it from side to side and note the long arc made by the racket head. The conjunction of arm and wrist movement provides the primary source of power in a squash stroke. Contributory power can also be generated by transferring the weight from the back foot to the front one. If the swing is vigorous enough this should happen in any case. The same is true of pivoting from the waist and hips, the fourth source of power.

But remember that your primary objective is control, not power. Most beginners find that hitting a backhand is considerably more difficult than a forehand. This is because the backhand is a much less natural movement. In the forehand, rather like a sideways throw, it is quite natural to turn the shoulders so that the back of the left shoulder faces the target. If the technique is repeated when playing backhands, the beginner will find less difficulty, and eventually, more often than not, the backhand is considered the better of the two swings.

By adopting a sideways-on position and taking note of the ingredients, you will have all the power you need. You need not strive for it. Once control has been achieved, you can learn to hit the ball harder.

The swing

The swing itself is composed of the backswing, the downswing and the follow-through, and although each needs to be considered separately, it is important to realize that they are all part of one continuous movement. The swing should be as long as possible without interfering with an opponent or endangering him in any way.

The easiest way to achieve this is to take the racket back so that the shaft is vertical to the floor. This also ensures that the wrist remains cocked. When the racket reaches the top of the backswing it will be high above the head and ready for the downswing. In the downswing the racket is brought down rapidly to meet the ball and the wrist begins to rotate. For in order to drive the ball forwards on to the front wall, the racket head must travel through the ball in a horizontal plane for some time in the hitting area. At impact the racket face is slightly open. After striking the ball the swing will continue on a fast upward path

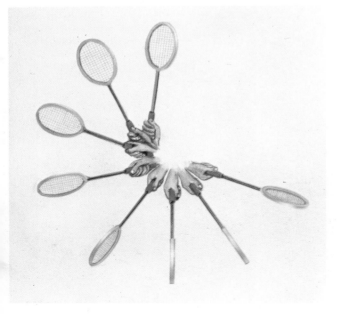

and the wrist will have completed its rotation. The follow-through will be complete when the racket head is held high above the head.

Forehand and backhand

In the basic forehand and backhand strokes the point of impact should be just in front of the body, and the ball should be struck between knee and ankle height most of the time. Now, in order to do this, you must bend the knees. Bending low may seem superfluous because it is perfectly possible to hit the ball without stooping. But the tendency will be to lose the sideways-on position and this will cause the wrist to drop. The result will be that the stroke will be weaker and accuracy will be lost.

One of the stock shots of the squash player (and one of the most difficult) is the drive which is played from close to the side wall, onto the front wall and back down the side wall. Practising this shot by yourself on both the forehand and backhand side will help groove the swing and will be the first step towards improving your play. Begin by standing just in front of the short line and move to just behind the service box as you grow more proficient. After a while you will be able to manage this without difficulty and you will be able to keep a rally going.

When you have mastered these two basic strokes, you are well on your way, because a squash match can be won with just these two strokes. The other strokes are really only variations of the forehand and backhand. Because it is possible to win with such a limited range of strokes, it follows that it is of paramount importance to perfect these basic strokes before proceeding to the more difficult shots. Although these new shots can be infinitely more satisfying when they are performed well, the temptation to progress on to them too quickly should be resisted. It is important to first consolidate the gains made by practising the basic strokes.

◄ This player has been forced to 'boast' from the back corner (see p. 35) but the technique for his backhand remains the same. Note the high follow-through.

Varying the stroke

Having practised and perfected the basic strokes of the game we can now go on to look at some interesting variations. The first and most important is the drop shot, while the lob, volley, half-volley and boast are useful additions to every player's repertoire. A knowledge of the different approaches to serving—lob, overarm and backhand —is also important.

The drop shot

The drop shot is a short shot which hits the front wall just above the board and bounces on the floor very close to the front wall. It is probably responsible for more winning shots (and more losing ones) in club squash than any other. Played correctly, it is the most devastating shot; played carelessly, it can be the losing shot in a game. Your success will depend upon your ability to perfect and use the drop shot sensibly.

Everything in the preparation of the drop shot should be identical to the drive, except for a slightly shorter backswing. Power is unnecessary. Accuracy is essential. In the downswing the racket face is much more open on impact than for the drive, and travels under and slightly across the ball.

The spin which results is important. It enables you to swing the racket through the ball much more quickly without increasing the pace of the ball. That also, adds a little bit of deception, which will keep your opponent guessing.

The follow-through should be almost as long as for the drive. While this may not seem entirely necessary at first, it will help to prevent the fault of not being definite enough. Too often the stroke is checked near impact and not enough racket-head speed is generated. The result is that the ball hits the board, or even worse, the tin.

Bending the knees is critical if you are to get your racket under the ball. Apart

▶ The effect of cut on the ball. The racket head begins its path through the ball from above and finishes below. The ball rotates as it moves forward. When it makes contact with the wall, the downward path of the ball as it loses pace is exaggerated and it hits the floor more quickly. More pace is lost as a result and the second bounce of the ball is closer to the front wall.

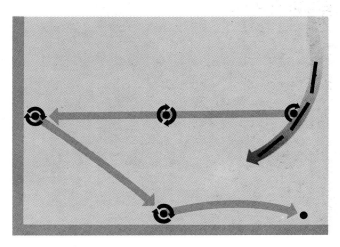

from being a technical requirement, it will also help you to watch the ball very closely. The final product should be a stroke which can best be described as an underhit drive.

The drop is generally played from the front of the court, when your opponent is behind you. It calls for deftness and, above all, accuracy. Consequently it is a difficult shot to attempt from the back of the court, because the ball has to travel much further.

However, this is not to say that the drop from the back is forbidden, merely a caution to exercise discretion. You can sometimes surprise your opponent sufficiently to make the shot very effective. But be sure you can make it accurate. Practice is the only way.

The reward for the effort is to see your opponent struggling to the front wall in pursuit of your drop, and relishing the winning shot which will follow. Without doubt the drop is the most satisfying shot in the game.

The lob
The lob is a shot which rises after hitting the front wall so that it clears your opponent's head, landing in the back court as near to the back wall as possible.

In the majority of cases the lob is used from defensive, forward positions. If it is played from too far back, the ball must strike the front wall high—nearer the out-of-court line—in order to clear your opponent. There

is an obvious danger of the ball hitting the side wall above the out-of-court line. In the forecourt a well-played lob can gain time if you are out of position. As an attacking weapon it can unbalance an opponent who anticipates the drop.

The technique is not dissimilar to the drop. Prepare with a full backswing so that

▲ Playing a drop shot. The open racket face imparts spin, causing the ball to drop quickly downwards.

you don't give any indication of your intentions. Bring the racket down in the same way as for the drop, but keep the racket face well open to give lift. The stroke will need

▼ The ideal trajectory of the perfect lob. From well forward in the court (where the player has the option of a drive, a drop or a lob), this lob would clear any opponent's head. If the speed is also correct, the ball will die into the back wall, after touching the side wall, making any worthwhile reply impossible.

But note how far the ball travels above the out-of-court lines. Keeping the ball in play therefore demands that the angles be judged nicely. The problem is accentuated when you play the lob from further back in the court, for in order to clear an opponent from this position you will have to hit the front wall very close to the out-of-court line.

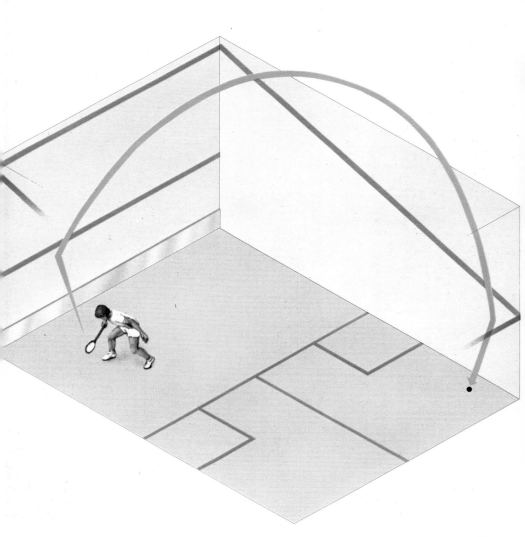

to be firmer than for the drop as the ball must travel to the opposite rear corner in a diagonal arc. The ideal shot will kiss the side wall on its downward path to the floor, dying into the back corner. It will definitely not hit the back wall first, as this will cause the ball to rebound into mid-court. You will then be at a severe disadvantage.

Of course, when you are at full stretch it will be impossible to maintain this technique, and the natural tendency of any player in this position is to scoop up the ball in a last minute lunge to play the ball before the second bounce. However, try to bear in mind the length and height of the ideal lob even when you are under pressure.

Always remember, too, that the ball must clear your opponent. A good player will try to intercept anything short by volleying.

The volley

The volley is a stroke played before the ball has bounced. It is generally an attacking shot, although for developing players it will have the added advantage of avoiding difficulties with the back wall and corners. For this reason alone it is advisable for any player to volley whenever a clear opportunity arises. A later section discusses more fully the reasons for taking this course.

The technique for volleying is the same as for driving with small modifications for height. In the case of the low volley it is identical: side-

ways-on, a full backswing, wrist cocked and the same arc of swing.

But if you wish to volley at, say, waist height, the kind of swing used in driving must be altered to describe a much shallower arc. The higher the ball is taken, the more the shape of the swing is changed.

But it is important to realize that with all kinds of volleys the principles remain the same. There is a natural tendency to strike the ball

▲ A shoulder-high volley. The player has taken a full backswing from a sideways-on position.

with slice, but take care not to impart this spin deliberately. The aim should be to strike the ball as 'flat' as possible, although some spin in is almost inevitable.

Once again it is important to realize that accuracy is the key. Without it the shot will be wasted. So always ensure that you are well balanced before you volley and that you are not stretching too violently.

The half-volley
Strictly speaking the term 'half-volley' is a misnomer as the ball is played immediately after the bounce on the floor. This may not be a common shot, but it often has the advantage of expediency, since it is generally played as a reflex action, or to save embarrassment to oneself, or to cause it to an opponent.

In a case where the ball bounces at almost the extremity of a player's reach, the basic principles can only apply if the player gets as low as possible. However, when the ball bounces very much nearer to the player—right at his feet, for instance—then it is impossible not to drop the wrist.

Too often the club player uses the half-volley as a convenience shot, not bothering to move his feet for a volley or a normal drive. Because accuracy is difficult to achieve with a half-volley, the extra effort is often worthwhile. For the same reason, try to restrain yourself from the all-out slog on the half-volley.

The kill
The kill is a shot which is played from a drive. The ball is struck at the top of the bounce and hit as close to the top of the board as is prudent. The ball is also hit considerably harder than for a regular drive. The result is

that the ball, already low when it hits the front wall, bounces twice in a space close to the front wall.

Side-wall shots
So far we have dealt with strokes which are played directly to the front wall. The angle and the boast are two shots which hit the side wall nearest to the player before hitting the front wall.

The angle
The angle is an attacking stroke generally played from the middle or front of the court. The object is to play the ball around the walls so that the ball 'dies' into the

opposite side wall. It is totally ineffective if the ball bounds back into the court, so a sound knowledge of the angles and experience of pace and height are of the utmost importance. However, when played perfectly the angle can manoeuvre an opponent out of position or be the killing shot when a player is already a long way from the front wall.

▼ Caught on the hop, the player has to improvize a half-volley to keep the ball in play.

The boast

In the early career of the squash player the boast will be used most frequently when trouble looms in the back corners. For even the most accomplished player it is sometimes the only way to keep the ball in play. In this instance the stroke is very definitely defensive and is only a means of prolonging the rally. But there are occasions when the boast can be used as an offensive weapon. In ·either case a sound knowledge of the angles is necessary and this can only be learned by experience.

The technique for the stroke is identical to that of the drive, except, of course, that in order to dig the ball out of the corners you cannot face the side wall. You should face the corner, because the direction of your shot will be into the side wall, not the front wall. Don't get too cramped in the corner and inhibited by the proximity of the two walls. You must leave yourself room to make a full swing at the ball, even though the first two or three times you make a full-blooded swing in the corner you will probably be wondering about the cost of a new racket.

You will also have to alter your aim somewhat. The tendency with beginners is to hit the ball down when boasting. Make sure to aim higher with your stroke and to hit the ball firmly, because it will bounce into the wall shortly after leaving your racket, losing much of its pace as it travels.

The back-wall boast

Aiming high is even more important when hitting a back-wall boast. This stroke is rarely used. Ideally it should never be played because the result gives an opponent a great advantage at the front of the court. But there are occasions when it is the only means of keeping the ball in play. Usually the ball is played directly from the back wall to the front, although there is nothing to stop it hitting one of the side walls on the way.

Serving

All rallies must start with a service. Remembering that only 'hand in' can score a point, the server in squash has an advantage. It is not so marked as in tennis, where sheer power or accuracy can force a service winner, but nonetheless the opportunity must be taken to put your opponent in as much difficulty as possible.

Faults

Before dealing with the various ways of achieving this, let us first consider 'faults' or foul services. The rules provide for two kinds of faults. The worst kind will lose you the rally immediately and the other allows you another chance.

You transgress in the first category if your serve does any of the following.

1 Hits one of the side walls or the floor before the front wall.

2 Hits any wall above the out-of-court line, including the ceiling.

3 Hits the front wall below the board.

One last embarrassing way to become 'hand out' is to miss the ball completely while attempting to serve.

Faults in the second category occur for the following reasons.

1 If one of the server's feet is not wholly within the service box.

2 If the ball strikes the front wall below the cut line but above the board.

3 If the ball lands outside the opposite back quarter (although the ball may

▼ The more forward of the two players could have played a straightforward drive from this position. Instead he has chosen the more adventurous angle, which demands that his opponent must cover the maximum distance to retrieve the ball.

As always the theory is simple, but the practice is fraught with difficulties. Imperfectly played, the angle can set up an opponent's winner or immediately lose the rally by being too soft or too acute. Do not be discouraged if your first attempts meet with disaster. Use it sparingly to match play to begin with until you have had enough practice to be confident that you can produce the result you want. For all the difficulty, the angle is one of the most exciting strokes in the game.

never reach the floor if the receiver chooses to volley).

In all cases the receiver may elect to take the service, in which case the service becomes good. Of course, two consecutive faults will lose the point. Finally a reminder that in squash the lines are 'out'.

Lob and flat serves

Now to return to making life difficult for your opponent. Your first objective is to deprive him of the luxury of the volleyed return, unless you can make the ball hit the side wall first. There are two basic methods to use. They are the lob service, which is effectively the same as the lob itself, and the hard, flat service. The first has the advantage of being more damaging when produced accurately, but the disadvantage of flirting with disaster in the shape of the out-of-court line. The second is much safer.

In either case the aim should be to hit the side wall at the back of the service box. The lob service should prevent the volleyed return because of height; the flat service should rely on speed and a lower trajectory.

Your other main objective should be to keep the ball as close to the walls as possible. If the ball rebounds into the middle of the court, then you will allow your opponent too many alternatives.

Most services are delivered on the forehand side, although some players find

it easier to make the ball hug the wall by serving backhand from the forehand (or right) service box. Variety is essential and changes of pace and direction can give you an advantage. It is worthwhile trying the odd sharply angled service, although you may not be able to control the T if your opponent is alert.

For the same reason, surprise, you might try a service which is aimed directly at the receiver. In a recent international match this ploy worked for Gawain Briars, much to his delight.

It follows from what has been said about serving that the best place to receive the serve is in the middle of the back quarter. From this position you will be able to step forward to a service which is not going to hit the side wall at the correct point; or step back for a well delivered service.

This is the full range of strokes needed to play the game of squash. But they have been examined in isolation and without introducing the one thing which makes squash the dynamic game it is: movement.

Three variations of the service.
◀ **1** Here the player has lifted the ball to the front wall from around waist height in a lob serve. He will rely on accuracy, not pace, to make life difficult for his opponent.
▲ **2** The flat serve is played from nearer shoulder height to gain a little more power.

▲ **3** The backhand service is sometimes easier to keep close to the side wall.

▶ In all cases you should aim to bounce your service on the side wall just behind the service box. The height at which the ball hits the side wall will depend upon the type of service you have employed. If you succeed in placing your service accurately, your opponent will be pinned down to the corners and you will be in immediate control of the rally.

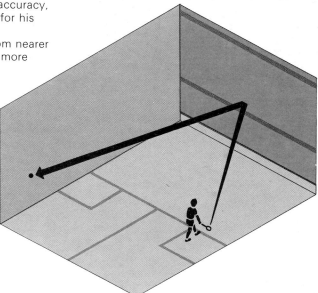

Fundamentals
of movement

Even though you might be able to produce perfect
strokes when practising, you will have achieved
nothing if you don't observe the fundamentals of
movement about the court. It will become evident
later that the squash player's prime objective is to
move his opponent around the court. The manner
in which he does this is the subject of a later
section. If you in turn are to be moved around the
court you must take heed of four fundamentals:
watching the ball, footwork, balance and being in
a position of readiness.

Watching the ball

It is of course obvious that a player of any ball game would need some kind of divine assistance to be able to play without recognizing this first fundamental. Yet it is not only when you are playing a stroke that this rule applies.

As far as your own stroke is concerned, the timing and the quality will be better if you watch the ball right onto the face of the racket. Many players leave the last foot or so to instinct. This can develop into a bad habit. A good habit to get into is to keep the head down and over the ball at the point of impact.

After you have played your stroke, keep your eyes riveted to the ball until it hits your opponent's racket, particularly if your opponent is behind you. The importance of watching the ball in this way cannot be stressed enough. By watching your opponent play the ball you will gain valuable advance warning of his intentions. In consequence you will be able to set off earlier in the direction he has played the ball. This will mean more opportunities to hit winning shots or more balls retrieved from what would previously have been winning shots against you.

The other important reason for watching the ball in this way is safety. Many players new to squash keep their eyes on the front wall while their opponents are playing. Turning to look for the ball after it has been played can often result in a nasty eye injury.

▼ (Below) Both players' eyes are rivetted to the ball. (Opposite) The footwork of the player in the foreground allows him to make the perfect stroke.

Footwork

While practising the basic drives, the player has learned to keep his feet sideways-on to the front wall. Unfortunately, because your opponent will put you under pressure at times, it will be impossible to get into a perfect position every time you play.

The most common result of this pressure is to play the ball with an open stance. In other words you lead into the ball with the wrong foot (left foot for the backhand and vice versa). Whilst this may not cause you to miss the stroke, it will certainly deprive you of power, since you won't be able to pivot from the waist, and you will be relying on the strength of your swing and wrist snap. Because less power is lost on the forehand side, many players continue to play forehand from an open stance, even when they could correct their footwork in time to make a technically correct stroke. But the options open to this kind of player are slightly reduced, and the weapon which you will come to later, deception, can be lost.

In all cases, therefore, you should strive to reach the ball with the front foot leading into the stroke and in plenty of time. This means setting off as soon as you are sure where the ball can be struck most comfortably or to the best advantage. And it will also mean adjustment to correct overrunning the ball or arriving too late to make the best contact.

Balance

Closely allied to the fundamental of footwork is that of balance. Clearly it is no use hitting a stroke if you are off balance because you will again lose pace and possibly direction. There are so many

moving parts in any stroke: legs, arms, racket, ball. But at the moment of impact the forward movement of the body should be checked. In other words, although you step forward a pace with the leading foot, you do not continue the movement by bringing the back foot through in a walking movement. You should be rock solid on the front foot, with the back foot merely acting as an aid to balance. In this way you are maximizing your potential for speed and minimizing your chances of mishitting.

There is another aid to balance which is often neglected and that is the free arm. Female gymnasts on the beam sometimes have to use their arms to correct bad balance and you can use your free arm in the same way.

One further result of bad balance on the squash court is that if you have played a shot off balance, the recovery time will be longer. You will not be ready to set off for the next shot as quickly.

Readiness

It stands to reason from what has been said that you should at all times be alert and balanced, so that you are ready to set off wherever your opponent sends you. (At the time you should be

slightly crouched, knees bent, and have your wrist cocked so that you are prepared for the next stroke.)

Return to the T

It also makes sense that the place on the court from which it is easiest to retrieve any shot that may be contrived is the junction of the half-court line and the short line, the T. From here it is possible with one long stride to reach all but the very best

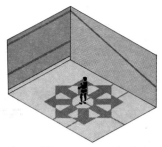

shots. The command of the T is thus the most important feature of competitive play. From here it is possible to

dominate the pattern of the game. After every stroke you should head for the T. The further away from the T you are when your opponent makes his shot, the further you will have to run. The further you are away when you play, the more time you will need to regain your position at the T.

▼ Even though the player in the foreground is at full stretch for this backhand, he is still well balanced.

Anticipa-tion

In observing the four fundamentals of movement, you will have taken a giant step towards improving your game. There are several other beneficial factors which will follow as a completely natural consequence of these fundamentals.

You may wonder how it is that the top players are able to reach shots which to the layman are near perfect drop shots or angles, and in some cases reach them with ease. Conceding a little in speed and fitness is not enough of an explanation.

Watching one player alone rather than the rally he is playing provides the clue. After playing the ball the top players immediately move towards the T. As their opponent moves to make a reply, they may have many options open to them. But if their options are restricted, then the non-striker knows that the ball can only be played in a particular way and can only end up in a particular place in the court. He is therefore able to move to the place where he expects the ball to arrive even before his opponent has hit the ball.

This intelligence is gained as a result of experience, but can never be achieved if you do not watch the ball *even when your opponent is playing*. By watching him play the shot you will also glean valuable information about the pace and exact direction of the shot, and that of course, is invaluable.

Consequences

The result of all this gathering of information is that you have more time to prepare your stroke because you have set off in plenty of time. Conversely you have also restricted the time available for your opponent to play and that may turn out to be a decisive advantage in a rally.

The most obvious example of anticipation would be the case of a good length

◀ Qamar Zaman, one of the world's most exciting shot-makers.

drive down the wall which forces an opponent to boast the ball out of the back corner. You see that it is the only possible reply because of position, and accordingly set off for the front wall immediately.

One of the consequences of good anticipation is that you will not have to run so far. Another will be that you will sometimes never actually reach the T. While this may seem to contradict one of the fundamentals, the important thing to remember about the T is that, while it is not absolutely necessary to occupy the T between strokes, it is totally vital to return there as quickly as possible after playing your stroke. In a down-the-wall rally, you may never actually get there, because the ball never leaves the wall and the only possible safe reply from

your opponent is to repeat the drive.

For the most part you will find that you never actually occupy the T, merely pass through it on your way to playing another stroke, or start to move towards it but anticipate your opponent's next move. In fact the only time you can be certain of T occupation with a little time to spare, is after serving. In most other cases the distance to travel is too far to dwell on the T.

Perhaps the most important consequence of the conjunction of the fundamentals is that a more perfect stroke is possible more often. The more pressure you find yourself under the less effective the stroke is likely to be. First footwork, then balance and watching the ball falter if you have to stretch yourself to the limits when re-

▲ Moving to the T.

trieving. Gradually as tiredness sets in, your willingness to return to the T will diminish.

Accuracy and control

The more strokes you can play without such pressure the better, because you can achieve accuracy and control. No matter how much power you are able to generate, it will be of no benefit if the shot you play is inaccurate. Strive for a balanced, controlled swing at all times.

There is only one time when accuracy ceases to be of prime importance and that is when you are quite certain that your opponent has anticipated your stroke. If you are then able to change your stroke at the last minute and send it in another direction, only the general direction is important.

Deception

In the very highest class of squash, speed and stamina are priceless and essential assets. Theoretically, if you are quick enough, it is possible to run down anything but the perfect nick shot (see p. 50). But in practice, even the swiftest and most agile retriever can be outmanoeuvred by an opponent who can feign one shot while intending another. Because he has anticipated one shot, the retriever is wrong-footed and has to travel further in less time. The result of the deception is often to put the retriever at a decisive disadvantage.

Deception shots

There are many ways and many situations in which to practise deception. The most effective place is in the fore-court, because from here the ball has less distance to travel, whatever the shot. But do not neglect to try it on occasion from the rear of the court. At the very least it will have the element of surprise, and, although your opponent may retrieve the ball comfortably, you will have kept him guessing and, perhaps more important, stopped him taking advantage by anticipating your shot.

Methods of deception

The easiest and most common method is to show one shot while intending and playing another. And by delaying the stroke to the last minute the full effect of the deception will be realized. It will sow seeds of doubt in your opponent's mind. If he has recovered quickly to the T, it will cause him to stop and he is likely to be back on his heels. And finally, if he

has started the wrong way, it is much more tiring for him to stop, turn, and begin again, this time in the correct direction.

Another way is to alter the direction of the shot at the last moment by changing the position of the wrist. Players with strong wrists can prepare for a straight-forward drive down the wall and change it into a cross-court drive by bringing the wrist through more quickly. Alternatively you can shape to play a drive and slow the downswing, turning the shot into a drop. However, these methods are fraught with difficulty and in some cases run contrary to the basics of stroke production. The most common fault when using the wrist as a means of deception is that the wrist will drop, and this increases the chance of error.

None of these methods should be attempted unless you are able to get to the ball and be in a good position. In many ways the chance to practise deception is the reward for good footwork.

Finally, remember that this is a reasonably advanced technique and should not be attempted until you are proficient at the bread-and-butter strokes.

▼ From the front of the court all things are possible. The safest shot is the straightforward drive down the wall (purple). The drop (orange) could be an immediate winner and the lob (blue) could embarass an opponent who comes forward precipitately. Finally the angle (green) affords a fourth option.

But that is only half the story. You have a choice of four shots on the other side of the court: cross-court drive, drop, lob and reverse angle. With all these you should be able to keep your opponent guessing.

Remember to try to leave your shot until the last moment—and you can only do this if you arrive in plenty of time for your stroke.

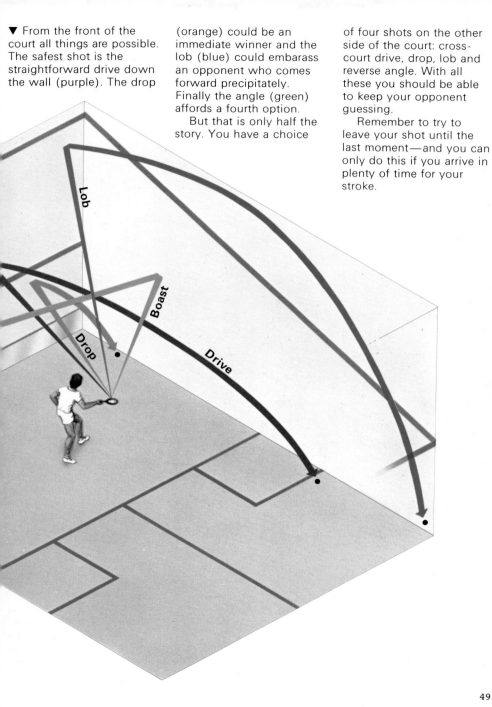

Lob

Boast

Drop

Drive

Basic tactics

At the heart of all ball games is the notion that one side has to try to put the ball—whether by foot, hand, bat or racket—out of the reach of the other side. Or at least to put the ball where it is difficult for the other side to achieve the same object. This is the most basic tactic of all, and in squash it is put into practice in several ways.

The nick shot

The nick is the crack where the side wall meets the floor. If the ball bounces on the floor before bouncing on the side wall, the path of the ball will follow an upward direction and vice versa. The nearer together the two are, the less marked the upward or downward direction. If the ball bounces on both wall and floor at the same time, the result is that the ball comes out horizontally. In effect, it simply rolls along the floor. This is the perfect squash shot because it is impossible to return.

While the nick shot is difficult (although by no means impossible or even rare), making your opponent run is a safer tactic by far. If the nick shot is missed and falls within easy reach of an opponent, you will probably find yourself on a long chase for the next shot. But there is no harm in trying for the nick, if at the same time you are asking an opponent to cover vast tracts of squash court. Do not neglect to practise the nick shot. You should attempt it whenever

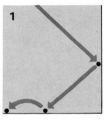 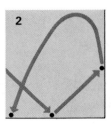 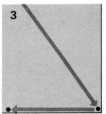

▲ Three different results from a ball hitting the side wall. **1** After hitting the side wall and then the floor, the ball will die reasonably quickly. **2**

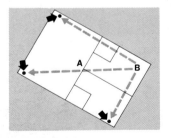

you hold the dominant position.

Playing to length

Shots played to length are the bread-and-butter diet of the squash player. The position of dominance attained by the player who occupies

Where the ball hits the floor first, the looping trajectory means the ball takes time to settle. **3** The result of the nick shot. Although the nick shot is by no means a rarity, it is better to err by making the ball hit the side wall first.

◀ Player B having just played, player A must aim his stroke to end up in any of the three corners. B will then be travelling the maximum distance.

the T has already been mentioned. The converse is also true, i.e. the further from the T a player has to move, the less dominant he is and the harder he has to work. If you have control of the T, your object should be to keep your opponent behind you until an opportunity for the short shot presents itself. If you do not control the T your aim should be to manoeuvre your opponent away from the T, so that you can occupy the space he has vacated.

This is achieved by playing to length. Length says nothing about how to play the ball, only something about where the ball should bounce. A perfect length ball bounces on the floor and dies into the back wall. Good length shots, however, must hit the back wall before bouncing for the second time on the floor. Anything which falls short is tending towards bad length, because your opponent must play the ball before it reaches the back wall. From such a position he can play an aggressive shot, even though he may be behind you and the T. By aiming for the perfect length ball there is little margin for error and in attempting such a winner, you may well fall short and present an opponent with the chance to counter-attack.

It is far better to err on the other side, for no matter how hard a ball is struck it will always be losing pace and falling from the back wall. Your opponent will therefore be obliged to play from close to the back wall.

There are many ways to play to length, the most common is the drive. Where the ball pitches on the front wall will depend on how hard the ball is struck, but in general terms it will be somewhere above the cut line if

▼ Chasing the length of the court to retrieve a drop shot.

you are standing behind the short line. The ball should pitch at the back of the service box or beyond. Obviously if you hit the ball softly you will need to aim higher up the front wall; and the nearer to the front wall you are playing, the lower you should aim. One of the dangers of playing a soft shot is that a quick opponent may take the opportunity to volley before the ball bounces to a good length.

At the same time as hitting to a length, you should of course try to keep the ball as close as possible to the side wall, so that your opponent not only has the back wall to contend with, but also the further restriction of the side wall.

Width

This brings us to another important topic: width. The player who occupies the T, although occupying a controlling position on court, cannot reach a ball which travels within a foot of the side wall in a single stride. Furthermore, if a ball strikes the side wall at or around the short line, it will be an ambitious player who attempts to play the ball at or near this point. He will have more room to play his stroke if he either takes it some time before or after it reaches the wall.

If you imagine that an opponent has driven you into the back corner, consider your best reply. You are unlikely to try an attacking shot such as the drop, because

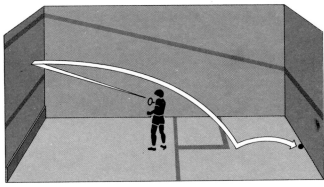

Length

Good length will depend upon where you are in the court, how hard you hit the ball, and where the ball bounces on the front wall. Three common examples are shown here.

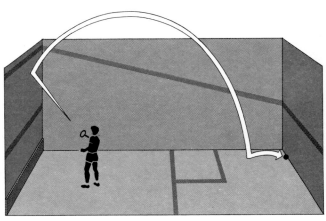

for one thing the ball has to travel the whole length of the court and you cannot guarantee to be accurate enough to produce a winner from that distance. If it is not a winner, your opponent should punish you. Remember you are in a defensive position and that your best riposte is to play for safety

Aim to play a drive so that its path both up and down the court is as close to the side wall as possible. If you have hit a good length then your opponent is unlikely to try and cut the ball out with a volley and will take the ball in the back corner. You will then have regained the initiative.

To continue this rally, suppose your opponent returns the compliment. Sooner or later one of you will play a ball which allows the other to attack or perhaps one will take the chance to hit crosscourt.

This tactic will certainly have the element of surprise. But the angles have to be understood and experienced before the perfect crosscourt shot can be played. In the down-the-wall drive, the position of your opponent will not deter you unduly. You are simply aiming to keep the ball as close to the wall as possible. But when playing the crosscourt drive the position of your adver-

sary is critical. If he is in front of the T your crosscourt shot must hit the side wall nearer to the front wall.

But let us suppose that he is in an orthodox position on the T. The place to aim the ball is low down on the side wall towards the rear of the service box, just the same as a hard service. In this way you have still observed the rules relating to good length and you will have driven your opponent into a corner.

There are two dangers with a less-than-perfect crosscourt shot. One is that

▼ The completion of one of the stock shots: the down-the-wall drive.

if the ball travels too close to an opponent before it reaches the side wall, he may, if he is quick, take the ball on the volley. On the other hand, if you correct that fault by making the ball hit the side wall too early, the ball will rebound conveniently into the court a long way from the side wall and you will have hit a bad length ball. From such a position you will have lost the initiative.

You will have gathered from what has already been said that to allow an opponent to volley is something to be avoided. The reason is simple. By volleying, the ball will not travel to the back wall. Therefore the player who volleys denies his opponent time. The length of

time that is saved will depend on the position from which the volley is played, but normally it will be from about the short line. The further forward a player is from the short line, the more time is saved and the greater pressure exerted.

Because this pressure can be decisive in a rally it is recommended that the chance to volley should be taken at all times when a good accurate stroke can be completed. If the volley is inaccurate, the object is lost.

For many players the volley is not a natural shot and they feel disinclined to play the stroke when they can opt for an easier drive. Such players should observe the rules concerning good length until they feel at

▲ Having played the cross-court drive, the player on the right moves to occupy the vacant T position.

home with the stroke. Later they will be able to introduce the crippling drop volley as an attacking weapon. You will remember how effective the drop can be. The drop volley can be doubly effective.

Short shots are an important part of the squash player's diet. While good length is the bread-and-butter, short shots are the jam, for very often they will be the final shot of a rally. But the short shot, like the drop, should only be attempted when you have been able to move your opponent out of position. By

▼ A well positioned opponent can easily deal with a less-than-perfect cross-court shot. He can step forward to intercept a shallow angle before it hits the side wall, or step back to play the wider angle after it has rebounded into the centre of the court.

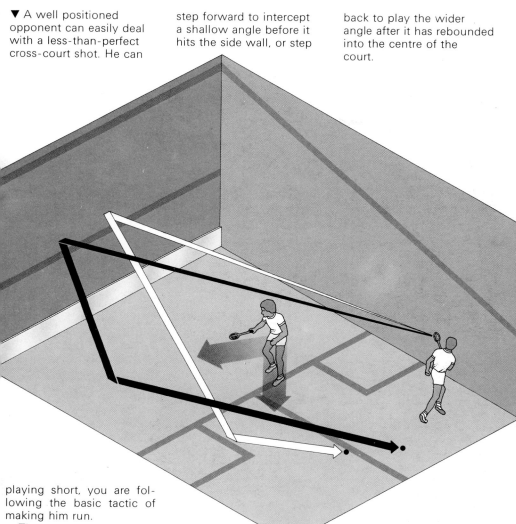

playing short, you are following the basic tactic of making him run.

There are many variations of the short shot. We have already discussed the drop and the angle (boast), to which you should add the reverse angle. This is similar to the boast in that it hits a side wall before it hits the front wall. But in this case it is the side wall furthest from the striker instead of nearest to him. Played from the front of the court the ball stays in the forecourt and often has the element of surprise in its favour, although at the highest level it is rarely played because it is very difficult to disguise your intentions.

With the reverse angle (as with the angle), the ball should end up dying into the opposite side wall. The same is true of the straightforward drop shot which, because it is easier to play, having no need of the correct angle, is recommended in preference. It has the advantage of being more direct.

Practice

If, like most squash players, you hate the thought of losing, you will want to take steps to remedy this situation, and the quicker the better. There is no substitute for practice.

Squash has an advantage in that you will be able to practise on your own and in many cases it is better for you if you do. The introduction of a practice partner frequently brings a competitive element to the session and if you are not very careful the value of the practice will be lost. However, where a suitable practice partner can be found, practice sessions can be made more varied and more fun.

Drives
The basic practice exercise must be hitting down-the-wall drives to a good length. Position yourself behind the service box and a little further away from the side wall. Hit your drives so that they bounce deep in the court and rebound from the back wall. In this way you should be able to keep a rally going and driving to length from the corners will become second nature.

You should begin this exercise (as you should with all practices) by using less pace than you would under normal match conditions. Concentrate very hard on accuracy so that you build up a rhythm. Once the rhythm is established you

can build up the pace.

In this exercise you will find some difficulty when you hit a good shot against yourself into the corner. If this happens try not to boast to keep the ball in play. Do your best to play a drive down the wall. If a boast is the only answer, call it a winner, stop the ball and start again.

Only use the boast if you want to add movement to your practice. Playing from a stationary position can become monotonous, so if you begin to tire of the exercise, hit the ball crosscourt and play two or three drives to length down the wall before driving crosscourt again.

Volleys
A good exercise for accuracy and ball control is to aim

▲ The basic practice for the down-the-wall drive to length. You should be able to keep a rally going by making the ball rebound from the back wall.

your drives so that they drop into the service box and continue rallying.

When that becomes easy you should make the target smaller, but it will take the beginner some time to keep the ball in the service box for even 50 per cent of the time, because the exercise demands not only that the length be right, but also the direction.

You should do both these exercises on both forehand and backhand wings. You can also use a variation to practise volleys. Aim your volleys for length but cut them out before the bounce and continue rallying. Both these exercises can be incorporated to form a practice with a partner. While the player behind the service drives down the wall to length, the forward player intercepts and volleys to length.

By standing some four feet from the front wall you can practise the drop into the corner. You should attempt to play a nick. Clearly from such a short distance you will be playing the ball very softly, but as your accuracy increases you can step backwards towards the T, keeping the rally going for as long as possible.

A similar exercise can be used to practise the angle. Beginning from near the T, play a forehand angle and move to the backhand wall to repeat with a backhand angle. This is a demanding practice both for accuracy and for movement.

An advanced practice is to play a forehand from the T into the front backhand corner, making sure that the ball hits the front wall first. The result will be that the ball should come back to you on the backhand side. You can then play a similar shot into the front forehand corner. This exercise improves your knowledge of the angles and, when you become adept, it is a good way of strengthening the wrist. Again, this exercise can be used for the volley.

Both these exercises take the form of a rally so it is easy to repeat the shot you

▲ By playing into the corners at the front of the court on both the forehand and backhand wings, strength of wrist and knowledge of the angles are improved.

wish to practise. Some of the other strokes you will want to practise need a little ingenuity in setting up and cannot be incorporated into a rally, because they are supposed to be winning shots. But you can practise the drop and the kill from the T by hitting the ball onto the front wall so that it bounces onto the side wall and returns to the T. You have thus set up the moving ball during a rally.

Boasts

Practising with a partner is the best way to practise boasting. While one player stands in the front corner, the other positions himself

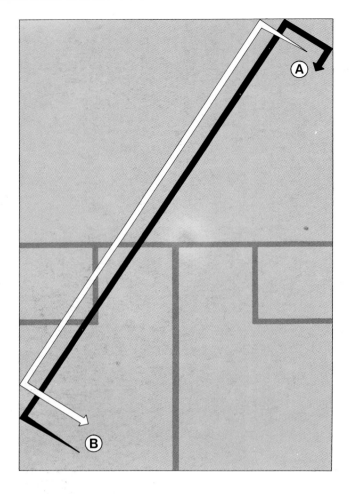

drive. The front player can sometimes play a drop to himself before driving.

The lob
Although there will not be as much pressure on the forward player as there would be under normal match conditions, a different routine can be used to practise the lob. Instead of driving the ball for partner to boast, lob the ball into the far corner. Partner is not allowed to volley the ball, but must wait to play after the bounce. If your lobs are good he will be forced to boast, and if they are very good he may well have to alter his position and play a back wall boast.

The nick shot
Never forget that the nick shot will win you a point outright. You should therefore devote a good deal of your practice time to perfecting this shot. If you are on your own you will need to set the ball up as outlined above. All shots should have a turn, especially the volley and the drop.

These routines will help groove the strokes that are letting you down in matches, but however well you can play them in your practice sessions there is no substitute for match conditions. So always finish up with a practice match with your partner. Only then will you be able to gauge any improvement in your weaknesses as they are tested in match conditions.

You should use the prac-

in the opposite back corner. From these positions, the front player drives the ball crosscourt and the back player boasts the ball so that it returns to the front corner. As this becomes a routine, the players should try to return as far as possible to the centre of the court. A form of fitness training will then have been incorporated into the exercise.

Variations of this exercise

▲ Practising the boast. Player A drives cross-court and B boasts the return.

will allow the players to use their down-the-wall drives and drop shots. The back player must travel across to the opposite back corner to retrieve the ball and should boast the ball on his opposite wing. The front player moves to the front corner to play another down-the-wall tice match as an extension of the practice session. Both you and your partner should be aware of the weaknesses you are trying to improve. The object should be to feed your practice partner with the kind of shots he wants to practise, while at the same time not making it so obvious that he expects the shot every time. It is a matter of striking the right balance between practice and match conditions.

Practising the service on your own can be a tedious business, so use the practice match to try out new variations, or improve your stock service. Nothing is more frustrating in a real match than to beaver away while 'hand out' to regain the serve only to give it away again by presenting the rally to your opponent with a poor serve. Some opponents will find difficulty with a hard, flat service and others with the lob service, particularly on their backhand side. So don't deprive yourself of the opportunity for a few quick points by having only one service in your armoury.

All these routines will quicken your improvement, but do not attempt to do them all in the same session. Thirty minutes of routine should be quite enough before going on to a practice match. Finally, for the last five minutes of the session, play a match flat out with no punches pulled. After a period of intense practice you deserve a few minutes of the real thing.

▼ Practising the cross-court lob. The opponent will boast the reply.

Match play

There are several factors which can give you advantages over your opponent, both before and during a match. Having a knowledge of your opponent and the court, being able to impose your game on your opponent and to concentrate constantly are just a few of the factors that can tip the balance of the game in your favour.

Pre-match advantages

Whether it is a representative league match for your club, a ladder or league within the club, or just your routine friendly, you are no doubt keen to do your best. Doing your best starts with your kit: be sure you are well turned out. This does not mean choosing the best equipment money can buy, but it does mean clean clothes and shoes. Although most clubs and centres have rules relating to clothing and footwear, in many cases they are flagrantly flouted and the courts are occupied by rugby players with squash rackets in their hands. Besides, being well turned out suggests that you mean business, and this may give you an advantage over your opponent.

There are one or two more things you can do before you go on court which may give you a few extra advantages. If it is at all possible, you should study your opponent so that you are familiar with his game. You should pay particular attention to his weaknesses and to his favourite shots when under pressure. Discovery of

the fragile features of his game will decide the areas you will want to attack. And knowing where he likes to play the ball when you have him on the run could mean that your anticipation has a head start and you will be able to conclude the rallies more swiftly.

If you are familiar with your opponent then you will have some idea of whether or not you think you are better than he. Try to ignore such thoughts. If you are better than your opponent it is enough that he will be at a psychological disadvantage. Do not throw the advantage away by being complacent. If you think he is better than you, take heart from one of the world's great sporting battlers, Pancho Gonzales. Before taking on an unknown in the first open tennis tournament at Bournemouth in 1968 he gave his opponent this friendly advice: 'When that ball comes over the net, it ain't got nobody's name on it.' The message is to clear-play every ball on its true merits.

Lastly, before you go on court, try to gain some

knowledge about the conditions. There are 'hot' courts and 'cold' courts. In the former the air is warm and the ball will fly faster. It will be more difficult to kill the ball and the rallies will last longer. The reverse is true on a cold court. Adjust your game plan to suit the conditions.

You and your opponent

Once you are on court you will have five minutes to knock up. During this time you should try to keep yourself as warm as possible. This will avoid accidents in the form of injured muscles in the early stages of the match. Stretching exercises in the dressing room are a good idea. Also you should study your opponent if you have not had a chance to do so before the match. But most important of all, you should concentrate on stroking the ball, so that your timing is sweet, and on hitting to a good length. You do not want to give your opponent the luxury of a few points' start simply because your length is awry.

The most obvious tactic in playing squash is to impose your game on your opponent, but it is often overlooked. If you can cope with the best that he can offer, you have no worries. This should always be your opening strategy and you need not change it if all goes well in the opening exchanges.

Attack your opponent's weakness by forcing as many errors from him as possible. However there is a danger that if you do this to excess you could lose the initiative for two reasons. One is that the weakness becomes a relative strength because of all the practice it is getting; and the other is that because your opponent realizes that you are giving, say, his backhand a pounding, he is able to anticipate the attack and in consequence has more time to compensate for his poor stroke. So vary your attack but give his weaknesses the majority of your attention.

Play the first few points as hard as possible. You want to give the impression that you are going to be hard to beat. The best way to achieve this end is to concentrate on making no errors and by playing to a good length. Aim the ball a few inches above the tin when playing your first short shots.

The initiative in squash can be lost in a very short time. A slight lapse in concentration can mean the loss of a succession of points and a total reversal of all that has gone before. Be aware at all times and keep a tight grip on your concentration. You must try for every point.

However, the scoring system allows for a difference in approach to the points depending on whether you are 'hand in' or 'hand out'. In the first case you will score a point if you win the

▼ Aim to dominate the T and the forecourt and keep your opponent behind you.

rally. It is therefore worth being a little more adventurous and you should try for the winner when you see a chance. On the other hand, at 'hand out' you should play more conservatively. Any error when attempting a winner will cost the point and no gifts should be distributed, even if you have a substantial lead. By making three quick mistakes after holding game ball at 8–0, your opponent will gain encouragement, and the long haul to retrieve the situation will not seem so arduous.

If everything goes well for you in the first game, then there is no reason to change your strategy, although many players will try something new in the mistaken belief that if they are better in one department of the game they must be better all round. But let us suppose that you are engaged in a tough struggle and that there is nothing much to choose between you both.

You should seek to tip the scales in your favour by finding a marginal edge somewhere. Often a change of pace will do the trick: mix powerful drives with softer ones and you may deceive by the slightly different trajectories of your shots. In any case you should always vary your game to keep your opponent guessing. Repeated patterns of play will only telegraph your intentions.

In these close situations you should also make a point of keeping an eye on your opponent between the rallies. Does he look tired or is he as strong as when he started? If he looks weary, increase your pace. For your part, try to give nothing away. If you are tired, try taking the pace out of the rallies by playing slow shots down the walls.

If the score reaches eight-all and you are 'hand out', remember to set to two (make the game to ten points). Although you will always be trying to make life difficult when you are 'hand out', there is no guarantee that you will be able to win the next point; the game will be lost if you opt instead for the 'sudden death' of a one-point finish. It is much more likely that you may win one of the next two rallies and you will then be back in the match. Having said that, it has not been unknown for a call of 'no set' to surprise the server so much that he has immediately lost the next point.

Finally, if you are not wining, and not even getting close, something drastic must be done. That means a change of strategy. Try to analyze in play where you are coming off second best and try to counter. Your first thoughts should be of length and width, of your position at the T, and of watching the ball closely. If that doesn't work, you will have to admit, reluctantly, that he was too good on the day.

◀ This is the view of your opponent you hope to see —buried in the back corner.

Fitness

Fitness is a key factor in squash and many people take up the game for just this reason. Others who have been recruited from other sports have a head start, but being fit for rugby or soccer does not necessarily mean that you are equipped to dash about a squash court for hours on end. A completely different set of muscles is being called upon. An obvious example would be the case of the soccer player who may be able to keep his legs moving, but finds that his wrist is not able to wield the racket after an extended period.

There are three kinds of training which will help your fitness: long-distance running, sprinting and interval running, and circuit training. Long-distance running will develop stamina but, because pace is sacrificed for endurance, sprints must be introduced into the training routine.

Interval running is possible in a confined space as well as an open space. Alternate sprinting and jogging over the same shortish distances (say between 25 and 100 metres) will aid strength, speed and stamina.

If you have only a small area to run in, why not try the potato race? Draw two parallel lines some 10–15 metres apart and place six small objects or 'potatoes' on one of them. Starting from the other line, sprint across to collect one of the items and return to deposit it on the starting line. Repeat until you have transported all the potatoes. The exercise should be repeated at intervals.

In circuit training several exercises are combined to give a series of demanding tasks which must be completed as fast as possible. Any of the exercises can be tackled separately if you feel your weaknesses lie in one particular area. None of the exercises described below needs any special equipment. More advanced and sophisticated routines can be attempted in a proper gymnasium.

1 Squat thrusts. In this exercise you begin from a press-up position with the body supported by the arms. The legs are brought forward so that the feet are as far forward as possible and then extended to return to the support position.

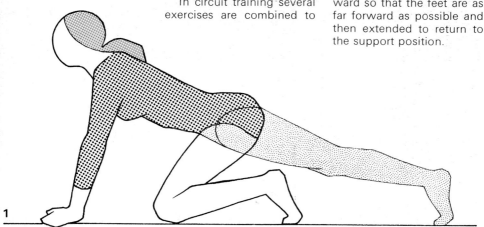

1

2 Sit-ups start from a lying position. With your hands clasped behind your neck, raise the body as far forward as possible so that the head is over the knees. Keep your legs as straight as you can.

3 Wrist-rolling needs a weight, some string, and an old racket handle. Attach the weight to one end of the string and the old racket handle to the other. With both hands roll the handle over and over so that the weight rises to the handle. Unravel the string so that the weight falls, and repeat.

4 Double knee-jumps involve leaping in the air as high as possible and bringing the knees up to hit the chest.

5 Step-ups need a bench or something similar. Simply step onto the bench, straighten to your full height and get down, always leading with the same foot.

6 Press-ups are invaluable in building arm strength, but really need no explanation.

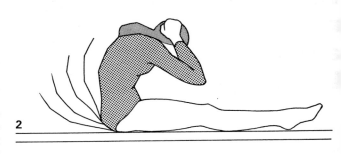

2

Circuits

For a circuit you will need to decide how many repetitions of each exercise you want to do. To set the standard, do as many of each exercise as you can in one minute. For the circuit, do half as many. Three circuits should be enough.

One word of warning. Before attempting any of these exercises, some of which are dynamic, you should do a few stretching exercises. Indeed, before you step on court you should go

4

through the same routine, gently stretching arm and leg muscles.

However, the most important aspect of training is to complete the exercise in the proper way. Remember that in training you are only competing against yourself and the benefits will be lost if you perform the routines in the wrong way. Remember also that physical condition is only part of the story. You will do better in the early stages of your development to concentrate on the skill of playing the ball accurately.

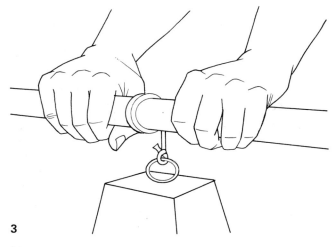

3

Referees, markers and court behaviour

In proper match conditions there will be two officials in control: the referee and the marker. It is a marker's job to call the score and to decide such issues as whether a ball is out of court or a foul service has been delivered. It is the referee's job to decide all appeals and to make decisions concerning fair play where the rules apply. His decisions are final, but you may appeal against some marking decisions. In most cases, however, the two officials are combined into one.

The job of the referee is an unenviable one because experienced and unscrupulous players can manufacture situations which could be construed as interference. The rule about this constantly uses such imprecise words and phrases as 'deliberate' and 'make every effort', and it is the referee's job to decide such issues as well as trying to decide whether or not a player has been prevented from making a winning return. It is difficult enough trying to disentangle the rule relating to interference when you are confronted with two scrupulously fair competitors, let alone when two villains are trying to con the referee into the award of an unwarranted penalty point.

Do not hesitate to ask for a let (see p. 66) if you think you are entitled to one. It is not considered at all unsporting. If it is an unjustified appeal you will simply be wasting your time in any case.

Talking on court

Some players will make comments between rallies which can sometimes be used to their own advantage. A passing quip about how well you are hitting your backhand drop is not a compliment but is designed to make you so conscious of your backhand drop that you will probably never hit another good one during the entire match unless you concentrate hard.

It is not a requirement, but many players call their own strokes 'not up', 'down' or 'out'. This is a laudable practice, but beware the 'sportsman' who calls them in the first game but not at eight-all in the fifth. The same applies to the player who might have been awarded a let in the early stages of a match, but decides not to appeal in the hope that the referee will make a mental note of his 'sporting' inclinations and treat him kindly later on.

Refrain from making any such comments yourself because you could upset your own concentration. If you have wind to spare you must be winning and then there is no need for talking. Your squash is doing your talking for you.

Time-wasting

Finally, beware of the player who wastes time when he is tired or short of wind, especially between games. The referee has the power to award a game to his opponent if a player persists in time-wasting after being warned. Time-wasting can take the form of a prolonged appeal to the referee or marker; taking overlong to retrieve the ball once a rally is finished; or making an undue fuss over mopping a wet brow or drying a wet hand.

Try to avoid all these ploys yourself. Play the game in the best spirit, otherwise you will not enjoy the game as fully as it was intended.

Lets and penalty points

You will remember that there are certain situations which cause a 'let' to be played. Before proceeding to the vexed and contentious issues concerned with fair view and freedom to play the ball, let us first detail the situations in which a let can be played.

A let shall be played in the following situations.

1 If in the course of a rally, a player turns on the ball and hits an opponent; or if, without turning, a player sends what would have been a good return towards the side wall, and it hits an opponent.

2 If a ball bursts during play.

3 If a ball bounces out of court after the first bounce on the floor.

In any of these cases the player has no need to appeal to the referee for a let, because it is automatically given. In all other cases a player must make no attempt to play the ball and should immediately appeal to the referee for a let.

The cases where a let may be allowed on appeal are as follows.

1 If the non-striker is unable to avoid the ball touching him before the striker has the chance to play (e.g. where the striker, being in front of the non-striker, masks the ball but allows it to pass behind him before striking).

2 If the ball touches any article on the court.

3 If the striker decides not to play for fear of striking his opponent.

4 If the striker, while playing a stroke, touches his opponent.

5 If the referee cannot decide an appeal or a marking decision, or where there is any doubt.

6 If ungentlemanly conduct causes an opponent to lose the rally.

7 When 'hand out' is not ready and refrains from taking the service.

8 If an appeal against a marking decision is upheld.

Interference

Inevitably when two players are rushing about in the confines of a squash court there are times when bodies will pass very close to each other. But it is a rule that at all times a player must endeavour to keep clear of his opponent. There are three situations where a player can cause interference.

1 If he obscures his opponent's view of the ball.

2 If he crowds the striker so that he cannot play the ball properly, or if such an excessive swing is employed by the striker that the non-striker is prevented from moving to the ball as he would like.

3 If he stands in a position which prevents his opponent from playing the ball to all of the front wall and the side walls close to the front wall.

Referees will frequently be called upon to decide such cases and they have the power to award lets and penalty points without waiting for an appeal. However, there are certain things to be considered before a let will be declined or awarded, or a penalty point given. They are best illustrated by the chart opposite.

Note that the only instance of a penalty point being awarded against you, is the situation where your opponent is in such a dominating position that he can hit a winner, always provided that you are making every effort to clear his path to the ball or his line of sight.

Did interference actually occur?

Yes	No	→	No let

Could obstructed player have reached the ball?

Yes	No	→	No let

What was opponent doing? Has he made every effort
to give fair view and freedom to play the ball?

Yes	No	→	Point

Could the obstructed player have made a winning return?

Yes	No	→	Let

Point

Players can unwittingly commit offences and it is the referee's job to decide when interference has occurred. It is therefore in your interests to 'make every effort' to avoid causing interference. If you don't, you are likely to cause your opponent to feel aggrieved at the treatment he has received. In many cases the match can degenerate into a contest for penalty points which is definitely not what was intended.

The photograph right shows the conclusion of a match between Kevin Shawcross and Torsam Khan which has gained notoriety as a classic of its kind. Unfortunately it was not the quality of the squash which gave it this reputation, but the brawling which developed as a result of one or other party feeling aggrieved.

Battle on the court

Although it is difficult to determine from photographs exactly who is responsible, we can at least guess at the misdemeanours of the two combatants from this sequence.

1 Torsam Khan has to move quickly past Shawcross to reach the ball, but in doing so is edging Shawcross out of the way before the shot has been completed.

2 The roles are reversed and Torsam's awkward position has been caused by Shawcross.

3 Shawcross is unable to move directly to the ball. Either player could be at fault here. Torsam seems to have completed his stroke and should be moving out of the way. Shawcross, finding his way, could perhaps have asked for a let instead of making contact.

5 Torsam makes a mockery of trying to avoid the big left-hander.

6,7 Shawcross shows his frustration.

1

4

5

Famous players

Every sport has its great champions. Sometimes these legendary figures can be described simply as having been the best exponents of their sport over a particular period. Others are remembered for having achieved their ascendancy by bringing some new technique to their game. Squash has champions who fall into both of these categories.

In squash the first great champions came from lands which had inherited the game from the British armed forces, in particular, Egypt and that portion of the Indian sub-continent which was to become Pakistan.

Amr and Karim

When Abel Fattah Amr (shown in the record books as F. D. Amr Bey) arrived in Britain in 1928 he did so as a tennis player attached to the Egyptian Davis Cup team and not as a squash player. He was persuaded to try squash as exercise when no tennis courts were free by Dan Maskell, at the time the coach for tennis, rackets and squash at Queen's Club, London. His aptitude for the new game was immediately apparent and he was so adept that Maskell recommended he play with the head coach and professional champion.

In three short years this Egyptian aristocrat became so good that he won the first of six British Amateur titles. The following season he had improved still further and added the British Open Championship and another 'Amateur' to his fast-growing list of titles won. From this time until his retirement he was never seriously challenged as the leading player. He won six

▲ A vintage picture of the great champion, Karim (left).

Open titles, although one of these included a year when he received no challenge from his rivals. (The Open was instituted in 1930 and from then until 1947 the champion had to accept at least one challenge each year. The contest was decided on a best-of-three-match basis.)

Amr was the first player to train for the sport. While others used squash as a useful aid to fitness in another sport or played just for fun , Amr took the game seriously and dedicated himself to winning. He was fitter than his

contemporaries, and through constant practice, his length was immaculate. He was not as talented a stroke-maker as some who were to follow, but he elevated the game to a new level. Anyone who was going to beat Abel Fattah Amr had to be able and prepared to run down every ball and be blessed with a special talent.

His game was precise without being spectacular. His one priceless quality was speed, and, being able to do

70

everything quicker, he outmanoeuvred his opponent. His dominance of the amateur world was such that it was said that he could probably give all but the best 7 points start and still win. In the event, no one defeated Amr, and when diplomacy dictated that he travel elsewhere, he retired. He was succeeded as the next of the great champions by his compatriot, Mahmoud el Karim.

Any similarity between the two Egyptians finishes there. For Karim came from a poor family. And while for Amr the game was a serious recreation, for Karim it was his livelihood. He was the professional at the famous Gezira Sporting Club in Cairo.

But for the intervention of the Second World War, Karim might have won more British Open titles than he did. As it was he won four, beginning in 1946 with the last played under the challenge system.

His was an exceptional talent. He was the complete strokemaker as well as being quick about the court. He hit the ball harder than Amr, and his temperament demanded he try for the most audacious winner whenever the opportunity presented itself. He was a stylist who made the game look easy, and as time went on he became better and better, winning more and more easily until the advent of Hashim Khan.

The Khans

There is in most sports a player who is recognized as the best. Like a Bradman, or a Pele. Of course, no one can be sure, for it is difficult to measure across bands of time. But against all that can be measured, Hashim Khan was the best.

▲ Hashim Khan.

Hashim was born in 1916 in Peshawar, Pakistan (as it became). As a small boy he used to sit on top of the walls of the old open air courts used by British officers in order to spot and collect the balls which went literally 'out of court'. In between times he would practise.

What he had practised became evident when he came to Britain in 1951. He hit the ball with terrific force, introducing a new dimension to the game. His technique was not precise in either of the ways in which Amr or Karim excelled. It was to exert maximum pressure with minimum risk and that meant thrashing the ball as hard as he could.

What he could also do which astonished the squash world was to return balls which were considered impossible. Hashim was short and had a barrel chest. (Some say that it was because of his chest that he was able to retrieve so well, being able to inhale great gulps of air.) If the occasion demanded, Hashim, forsaking all thought of dignity,

would quite literally run up the wall in order to retrieve a lost cause.

At his first attempt Hashim won the British Open, beating Karim 9-5, 9-0, 9-0. He was 35 years old, and although he was only six years younger than Amr, he had won his first major title exactly 20 years after the great Egyptian had won his first Amateur. He beat Karim again the following year and began a sequence of wins which lasted until 1957.

As Hashim became established as the best player around, he allowed himself the luxury of the attempt at a winner. Such was his affinity for the game that he virtually invented the nick shot, because it was he who was first able to perfect it. This additional weapon in his armoury was to serve him well as the years went by, for he was fast approaching 40 during his title-winning years.

▲ Roshan Khan.

Throughout this time he was founding a dynasty by introducing his brother to the game. Azam was rather fond of tennis and disliked his initiation at the hands of his elder brother. He was unable to complete one game when they first started, but gradually his fitness improved. The process started by Hashim in 1950 was completed in 1958 when Azam won the first of four consecutive Opens. Not surprisingly, being taught by Hashim, Azam played the same kind of game, and when the master left the stage to conquer new worlds, he carried on in the name of Khan, winning from 1958–61. (In 1959, an alteration in the month chosen for the 'Open' meant that Azam won two titles during the same year.)

In 1956 there had been an interruption to the trail blazed by Hashim and Azam. But the champion remained a Khan. A relative by marriage, Roshan, took the title by beating Hashim, who was having trouble with his shin muscles. That is not to belittle his performance, for it is generally recognized that Roshan was the third best of the Khans.

Roshan's family was perhaps more connected with squash than Hashim's, for Roshan's cousin was Abdul Bari, an Indian who had been Karim's final opponent in the 1950 Open. He also had a brother, Nasrullah, who was no mean performer and who was to play an important role in the development of another champion some years later.

Roshan's style was developed at Rawalpindi. He faced a certain amount of competition from his relatives, who tended to practise by themselves to the exclusion of Roshan. Indeed, there was a period before Roshan made his first trip to England (with only £5 in his pocket) when it seemed that the two brothers actively avoided a confrontation

▲ A latter-day Khan, but not a relative of the famous dynasty—Mohibullah, in 1979 rated world's number 3.

with him.

But although Roshan did manage to beat Hashim in the 1956 final, he is generally ranked third of the Khans. While he possessed very fine strokes, he was some way behind on fitness (being a smoker) and his match temperament was not as good.

The fourth (and last) of the Khans to make an impact was Mohibullah, who was a nephew to Azam and Hashim. He benefited greatly from being taught by them, although he was not endowed with their ability. Nevertheless he was a very exciting player and a great showman, who was never short of an audience to watch him play. When he made his first trip to this country in 1957, all the semi-final places in the British Open were filled by the four Khans. Mohibullah won the Open only once, in 1962, but he was three times runner-up to Azam, whose career was finished by an Achilles tendon injury.

By this time Hashim and Mohibullah had settled in America and were playing the hardball version of the game. Roshan had returned home to Pakistan and Azam had a post as coach to a club in London. When Mohibullah returned to England in 1963 to defend his Open title, Michael Oddy ended the Khan era, at least its international version. For in America the Khans had been winning the United States Open (later the North American Open) Championships since 1956. In fact, if you include Sharif, Hashim's son, who has spent most of his time in America, the Khans appeared in no less than 36 finals between 1954 and 1978 and have amassed 20 titles during that time. Lest it be thought that Sharif is the poor relation, his contribution outweighs all the others.

In modern squash the name of Khan still abounds. There is Torsam, Roshan's son and Rehmat, Nasrullah's son. But neither has reached the heights set by the earlier Khans. Strangely, another Mohibullah Khan, who is no relation, is the one most likely to put the name of Khan back on the roll of honour of the British Open. For since 1962, only one Pakistani name has appeared on it. The Khan dynasty, which lasted 11 years, is over.

Abou Taleb
Although Mohibullah had won the 1962 Open, his final opponent had already beaten Roshan in the semi-final and actually stood at match point in the final. His name was

Abou Taleb and in the following year he restored the Egyptian line to the squash throne. But there is a great question mark against Taleb's pedigree. Clearly Mohibullah was past his best in 1963. Not only was he 33, but most of his squash was now the American version. He rarely played the international game. Furthermore it is generally agreed that the standard of the professionals about this time was lamentable. The only serious opposition was therefore amateur and no amateur had won the Open since Amr.

▼ Abou Taleb, three times Open Championship winner.

Nevertheless, Taleb won the Open for three consecutive years (1963–5). His reign was abruptly halted by a phenomenon who was to change the face of the squash world: not only a new champion but a force that brought squash out of the 'dark ages' of its history and into the light beyond. He caught the imagination of the British public and spread the gospel of squash worldwide.

Barrington
Jonah Barrington started his competitive squash career later than most at the age of 23. Earlier he had led, by his own admission, a relatively debauched existence at Trinity

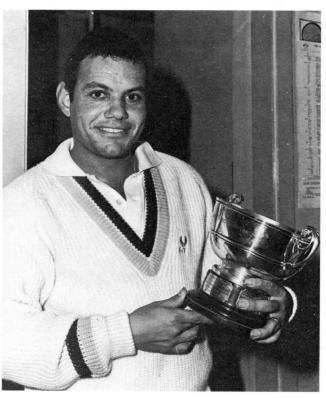

College, Dublin, and after failing his exams, his life lacked any kind of direction. A job at the SRA stimulated his desire to become a good player; a desire which became a consuming passion.

In 1965 Barrington dedicated himself entirely to squash, taking jobs which fitted his training plans, one of which included male modelling. He was advised and coached by 'Naz' Khan and later to a lesser extent by Azam. But after a year of hard effort he still could not survive the second round of the British Amateur, losing in straight games to the Egyptian, Shafik. A similar fate awaited him in the Open, where he lost to Boddington.

In the 1966–7 season Barrington became only the second player (and because of the changes he later wrought on the game) probably the last, to win both the Amateur and the Open in the same season. For good measure he gave a repeat performance the following season. In 1969 he turned professional, having

won three Amateur titles, although when he did so he was the only pro who played entirely competitively for his living. Later he was joined by Hunt, Hiscoe and Alauddin, and the beginnings of the professional tour was born.

Barrington compiled the most outstanding record apart from Hashim by winning six Open titles between 1966 and 1973. But the manner in which he achieved his success lifted squash to a new level. By making himself the fittest player in the world he demanded that in order to be able to compete, others should be at least comparatively fit, or suffer the consequences. For the early Barrington paid little attention to the subtleties of stroke-making. Length and line and a killing drop simply wore down his opponents until there was no more resistance. In doing this he often had to go through what he described as 'the pain barrier' several times. Thus he beat Dick Carter in the 1967 Amateur final. Leading 2 games to 1 and 7—4, Carter hit the tin going for a winner. Minutes later Barrington was home 9—7, 9—0. Carter could not move.

Barrington later realized that while he was trying to wear down opponents, he was giving the more talented of his

rivals the chance to beat him in straight games. It was then that he began to add to his limited repertoire of strokes. In that he studied and analyzed the game to an extent never before contemplated, Barrington became the complete player.

But history may regard his greatest contribution to the game the part he played in setting up the professional tour which now travels the world and in making the game popular at grass roots level. Barrington's dominance as effective world champion coincided with the boom in British squash. As if his competitive example was not enough, the Barrington 'clinics' have become famous and he has recently been appointed by the SRA to lend his wealth of experience to the aspiring younger generation.

Hunt

One of Barrington's great rivals was the Australian Geoff Hunt. They met in many monumental battles, two of which, in the 1969 and 1972 Opens, lasted a combined total of over four hours.

Hunt had been around when Barrington first came on the scene, although he is considerably younger. But Hunt started young and had captured his State Junior title at the age of 15 and a year later won the Australian Junior Championship. Another year saw him reach the final of the British Amateur. It was only the superiority of Barrington that precluded Hunt from compiling an astonishing record, for as Barrington declined Hunt took over.

Hunt had learned his lesson well. Apart from having a splendid range of shots, he worked hard on his fitness and in the inaugural World Open which was incorporated into the British Open in 1976, Hunt wore down the resilient Mohibullah Khan to win in five games. He has so far won six Opens, equalling Barrington's record and bringing him close to Hashim's all-time record of seven.

Another notable Australian player and a frequent sparring partner of Geoff Hunt is Ken Hiscoe. In 1962 he won the Amateur Championship and was the leading player in the Australian team which beat the British Men's team. Although something of a veteran now, he is still active on the competitive circuit.

The new Pakistanis

The next breed of champions looks like coming from the fertile squash-breeding grounds of Pakistan. Current ranking lists place five Pakistanis behind the world champion, Geoff Hunt.

Qamar Zaman has already fulfilled some of his vast potential by winning the British Open in 1974 and, although he is widely regarded as the most exciting stroke-maker in the game today, very

◄ ▶ Ken Hiscoe (left) one of the early influences on Geoff Hunt (right).

▶ Gogi Alauddin, former amateur champion.

often he is too headstrong for his own good. He introduced a new technique to the game by playing many shots with severe cut, which enabled him to play the kill more effectively and which caused the ball to pull up nearer the back wall on length shots. Geoff Hunt modified his technique to incorporate this new weapon into his game.

Zaman is currently ranked two, and close behind him is the man who is always associated with him, Mohibullah Khan. Zaman and Mohibullah emerged at the same time and were the first really new squash talent to burst upon the world scene for some time. Initially, Mohibullah was the better of the two, winning two British Amateur titles in 1974–5. Apart from a few minor titles, the years since then have seen him win mostly a series of second places. He has been runner-up in the British Open, the World Open, the Australian Open, and so on. But he is still young (23) and has time to prove himself.

Hiddy Jahan is the next on the ranking list, but he has been around for some time. He has never quite captured any of the really big titles, but is capable of beating anyone on his day. Such is the power of the man that he can dispense with the very best players in a matter of minutes if the mood takes him.

Where power is Jahan's most potent weapon, Gogi Alauddin's strength is his deft

◀ Heather McKay, the Australian who has dominated the sport since 1962.

▶ Janet Shardlow, still actively involved in the game as President of the WSRA.

78

touch. He floats balls around the walls. They look innocuous, but they are deadly. He won the British Amateur in 1971 and was runner-up in the British Open in 1975.

The last of the five is a newcomer, Maqsood Ahmed. Of the others there were great hopes for Bruce Brownlee of New Zealand and Roland Watson of South Africa, but neither has troubled the top group.

Morgan and McKay
In the history of squash there have only been two women who have dominated the sport. In 1948 and 1949 Janet Morgan (Shardlow) was runner-up to Joan Curry in the Women's Championships. For the next ten years she was to have no serious rival, and when the round ten was completed, she retired, deciding that there was nothing more to prove. She is the only player to have held the British, U.S. and Australian titles. Her supremacy was based on a seemingly endless ability to retrieve and it was rumoured that she was

the first woman to train specifically for squash.

If that record were not startling enough, a period of only three years was to elapse before the emergence of perhaps the greatest female sporting champion. Her name was Heather Blundell (later McKay). She had been tempted away from hockey at an early age, no doubt encouraged by her success at squash, which began in earnest when she won the Australian title at the age of 19. In 1962 she won the Women's Championship (regarded as the World Championship until an official event was started in 1976). Between those two dates she was not beaten.

What is even more astonishing is the fact that she only conceded 2 games in all that time.

Heather McKay was strong, although not excessively so. She was obviously very fit, although to judge by the length of her matches, she may not have needed to have been quite as fit as she was. She was also very quick, and was perhaps the most balanced in play.

In 1974 she turned professional and that seemed to signal the end of a remarkable competitive career. Most of her time was spent coaching in Canada with occasional exhibitions to keep her sharp. But the decision by the WSRA to make the game open gave Mrs McKay the chance to extend her domination — a chance she took with remarkable ease. One or two more games have been lost, but the superiority remains. Few athletes can have dominated their sport quite as comprehensively as this woman.

Rules

in accordance with the rules, the opponent wins the stroke. When hand-in wins a stroke, he scores a point; when hand-out wins a stroke, he becomes hand-in.

4. THE RIGHT TO SERVE

The right to serve first is decided by the spin of a racket. Thereafter the server continues to serve until he loses a stroke, when his opponent becomes the server, and so on throughout the match.

5. SERVICE

The ball before being struck shall be thrown in the air and shall not touch the walls or floor. A player with the use of only one arm may utilise his racket to project the ball into the air. The ball shall be served on to the front wall so that on its return, unless volleyed, it would fall to the floor in the back quarter of the court opposite to the server's box from which the service has been delivered.

At the beginning of each game and of each hand, the server may serve from either box, but after scoring a point he shall then serve from the other, and so on alternately as long as he remains hand-in or until the end of the game. If the server serves from the wrong box there shall be no penalty and the service shall count as if served from the correct box, except that hand-out may, if he does not attempt to take the service, demand that it be served from the other box.

6. GOOD SERVICE

A service is good which is not a fault or which does not result in the server serving his hand out in accordance with Rule 9. If the server serves one fault he shall serve again.

1. THE GAME, HOW PLAYED

The game of squash rackets is played between two players with standard rackets, with balls officially approved by the I.S.R.F. and in a rectangular court of standard dimensions, enclosed on all four sides.

2. THE SCORE

A match shall consist of the best of three or five games at the option of the promoters of the competition. Each game is 9 points up; that is to say the player who first wins 9 points wins the game except that on the score being called 8-all for the first time, hand-out may choose before the next service is delivered, to continue the game to 10, in which case the player, who first scores two more points, wins the game. Hand-out must in either case clearly indicate his choice to the marker, if any, and to his opponent.

NOTE TO REFEREES

If hand-out does not make clear his choice before the next service, the referee shall stop play and require him to do so.

3. POINTS, HOW SCORED

Points can only be scored by hand-in. When a player fails to serve or to make a good return

7. FAULT

A service is a fault (unless the server serves his hand out under Rule 9):

(a)
If the server fails to stand with one foot on the floor at least within and not touching the line surrounding the service box at the moment of striking the ball (called a foot fault);

(b)
If the ball is served on to or below the cut line;

(c)
If the ball served first touches the floor on or in front of the short line;

(d)
If the ball served first touches the floor in the wrong quarter of the court as that from which it was served or on the half-court line. (The wrong quarter of the court is the rear left for a service from the left-hand box, and the rear right for a service from the right-hand box.)

8. FAULT, IF TAKEN

Hand-out may take a fault. If he attempts to do so, the service thereupon becomes good and the ball continues in play. If he does not attempt to do so, the ball shall cease to be in play provided that, if the ball, before it bounces twice upon the floor, touches the server or anything he wears or carries, the server shall lose the stroke.

9. SERVING HAND OUT

The server serves his hand out and loses the stroke:

(a)
If the ball is served on to or below the board or out of court or against any part of the court before the front wall;

(b)
If the ball is not thrown in the air, or touches the wall or floor before being struck, or if he

fails to strike the ball, or strikes it more than once;

(c)

If he serves two consecutive faults;

(d)

If the ball before it has bounced twice upon the floor, or has been struck by his opponent touches the server or anything he wears or carries.

10. LET

A let is an undecided stroke and the service or rally in respect of which a let is allowed shall not count and the server shall serve again from the same box. A let shall not annul a previous fault.

11. THE PLAY

After a good service has been delivered the players return the ball alternately until one or other fails to make a good return or the ball otherwise ceases to be in play in accordance with the rules.

12. GOOD RETURN

A return is good if the ball, before it has bounced twice upon the floor, is returned by the striker on to the front wall above the board without touching the floor or any part of the striker's body or clothing, provided the ball is not hit twice or out of court.

NOTE TO REFEREES

It shall not be considered a good return if the ball touches the board either before or after it hits the front wall.

13. STROKES, HOW WON

A player wins a stroke:

(a)

Under Rule 9,

(b)

If the opponent fails to make a good return of the ball in play;

(c)

If the ball in play touches his opponent or anything he wears or carries, except as is otherwise provided by Rules 14 and 15;

(d)

If a stroke is awarded by the Referee as provided for in the Rules.

14. HITTING AN OPPONENT WITH THE BALL

If an otherwise good return of the ball has been made, but before reaching the front wall it hits the striker's opponent, or his racket, or anything he wears or carries, then:

(a)

If the ball would have made a good return and would have struck the front wall without first touching any other wall, the striker shall win the stroke, except that, if the striker shall have followed the ball round, and so turned, before playing the ball, a let shall be allowed;

(b)

If the ball would otherwise have made a good return, a let shall be allowed;

(c)

If the ball would not have made a good return, the striker shall lose the stroke. The ball shall cease to be in play, even if it subsequently goes up.

15. FURTHER ATTEMPTS TO HIT THE BALL

If the striker strikes at and misses the ball, he may make further attempts to return it. If after being missed, the ball touches his opponent, or his racket, or anything he wears or carries, then:

(a)

If the striker would otherwise have made a good return, a let shall be allowed;

(b)

If the striker could not have made a good return he loses the stroke.

If any such further attempt is successful but the ball before reaching the front wall hits the striker's opponent or his racket or anything he wears or carries, a let shall be allowed and Rule 14 (a) shall not apply.

16. APPEALS

(i)

An appeal may be made against any decision of the Marker, except for (ii) (a) and (b) below.

(ii)

(a) No appeal may be made against foot-faults.

(b) No appeal shall be made in respect of the marker's call of 'fault' to the first service.

(c) If the marker calls 'fault' to the second service, the server may appeal and, if the decision is reversed, a let shall be allowed.

(d) If the Marker allows the second service, hand-out may appeal, either immediately, or at the end of the rally, if he has played the ball, and if the decision is reversed, hand-in becomes hand-out.

(e) If the Marker does not call 'fault' to the first service, hand-out may appeal that the service was a fault, provided he makes no attempt to play the ball. If the Marker does not call 'Out' or 'Not Up' to the first service, hand-out may appeal, either immediately or at the end of the rally, if he has played the ball. In either case, if the appeal is disallowed, hand-out shall lose the stroke.

(iii)

An appeal under Rule 12 shall be made at the end of the rally.

(iv)

In all cases where an appeal for a let is desired, this appeal shall be made by addressing the referee with the words 'Let, please'. Play shall thereupon cease until the referee has given his decision.

(v)
No appeal may be made after the delivery of a service for anything that occurred before that service was delivered.

17. FAIR VIEW AND FREEDOM TO PLAY THE BALL

(a)
After playing the ball, a player must make every effort to get out of his opponent's way. That is:
(i) A player must make every effort to give his opponent a fair view of the ball, so that he may sight it adequately for the purpose of playing it.
(ii) A player must make every effort not to interfere with, or crowd, his opponent in the latter's attempt to get to, or play, the ball.
(iii) A player must make every effort to allow his opponent, as far as the latter's position permits, freedom to play the ball directly to the front wall, or side walls near the front wall.
(b)
If any such form of interference has occurred, and, in the opinion of the Referee, the player has not made every effort to avoid causing it, the Referee shall on appeal, or without waiting for an appeal, award the stroke to his opponent.
(c)
However, if interference has occurred but in the opinion of the Referee the player has made every effort to avoid causing it, the Referee shall on appeal, or may without waiting for an appeal, award a let, except that if his opponent is prevented from making a winning return by such interference or by distraction from the player, the Referee shall award the stroke to the opponent.

(d)
When, in the opinion of the Referee, a player refrains from playing the ball, which, if played, would clearly and undoubtedly have won the rally under the terms of Rule 14 (a), he shall be awarded the stroke.

NOTE TO REFEREES

(a)
The practice of impeding an opponent in his efforts to play the ball by crowding or obscuring his view, is highly detrimental to the game, and Referees should have no hesitation in enforcing paragraph (b) above.
(b)
The words 'interfere with' in (a) (ii) above must be interpreted to include the case of a player having to wait for an excessive swing of his opponent's racket.

18. LET, WHEN ALLOWED

Notwithstanding anything contained in these rules, and provided always that the striker could have made a good return:
(i)
A let may be allowed:
(a) If, owing to the position of the striker, his opponent is unable to avoid being touched by the ball before the return is made;

NOTE TO REFEREES

This rule shall be construed to include the cases of the striker whose position in front of his opponent makes it impossible for the latter to see the ball or who shapes as if to play the ball and changes his mind at the last moment preferring to take the ball off the back wall, the ball in either case hitting the opponent who is between the striker and the back wall. This is not, however, to be taken as conflicting in any way with the referee's duties under

rule 17.
(b) If the ball in play touches any article lying in the court;
(c) If the player refrains from hitting the ball owing to a reasonable fear of injuring his opponent;
(d) If the striker, in the act of playing the ball, touches his opponent;
(e) If the referee is asked to decide an appeal and is unable to do so;
(f) If a player drops his racket, calls out or in any other way distracts his opponent, and the Referee considers that such occurrence has caused the opponent to lose the stroke.
(ii)
A let shall be allowed:
(a) If hand-out is not ready and does not attempt to take the service;
(b) If a ball breaks during play;
(c) If an otherwise good return has been made, but the ball goes out of court on its first bounce;
(d) As provided for in Rules 14, 15, 16 (ii) (c), 23 and 24.
(iii)
Provided always that no let shall be allowed in respect of any attempt which a player makes to play the ball, except as provided for under Rules 15 and 18 (i) (d), 18 (ii) (b) and (c).
(iv)
Unless an appeal is made by one of the players, no let shall be allowed except where these rules definitely provide for a let, namely Rules 14 (a) and (b), 17 and 18 (ii) (b) and (c).

19. NEW BALL

At any time when the ball is not in actual play, a new ball may be substituted by mutual consent of the players, or on appeal by either player at the discretion of the referee.

20. KNOCK-UP

(i)

The Referee shall allow on the court of play to either player, or to the two players together, a period not exceeding five minutes immediately preceding the start of play for the purpose of knocking-up. In the event of a separate knock-up, the choice of knocking-up first shall be decided by the spin of a racket. The Referee shall allow a further period for the players to warm the ball up if the match is being resumed after a considerable delay.

(ii)

Where a new ball has been substituted under Rule 18 (ii) (b) or 19, the Referee shall allow the ball to be knocked up to playing condition. Play shall resume on the direction of the Referee, or prior mutual consent of the players.

(iii)

The ball shall remain on the court in view between games. Except by mutual consent of the players, knocking-up is not permitted between games.

21. PLAY IN A MATCH IS TO BE CONTINUOUS

After the first service is delivered, play shall be continuous so far as is practical, provided that:

(i)

At any time play may be suspended owing to bad light or other circumstances beyond the control of the players, for such period as the Referee shall decide. In the event of play being suspended for the day, the match shall start afresh, unless both players agree to the contrary.

(ii)

The Referee may award a game to the opponent of any player who in his opinion, persists, after due warning, in delaying the play in order to recover his strength or wind, or for any other reason.

(iii)

An interval of one minute shall be permitted between games and of two minutes between the fourth and fifth games of a five-game match. A player may leave the court during such intervals, but shall be ready to resume play at the end of the stated time. When ten seconds of the interval permitted between games are left, the Marker shall call 'Ten seconds' to warn the players to be ready to resume play. Should either player fail to do so when required by the Referee, a game may be awarded to his opponent.

(iv)

In the event of an injury, the Referee may require a player to continue play or concede the match, except where the injury is contributed to by his opponent, or where it was caused by dangerous play on the part of the opponent. In the former case, the Referee may allow time for the injured player to receive attention and recover, and in the latter, the injured player shall be awarded the match under Rule 24 (iii) (b).

(v)

In the event of a ball breaking, a new ball may be knocked-up, as provided for in Rule 20 (ii).

NOTES TO REFEREES

(a)

In allowing time for a player to receive attention and recover, the Referee should ensure that there is no conflicting with the obligation of a player to comply with Rule 21 (ii), that is, that the effects of the injury are not exaggerated and used as an excuse to recover strength or wind.

(b)

The Referee should not interpret the words 'contributed to' by the opponent to include the situation where the injury to the player is a result of that player occupying an unnecessarily close position to his opponent.

22. CONTROL OF A MATCH

A match is normally controlled by a Referee, assisted by a Marker. One person may be appointed to carry out the functions of both Referee and Marker. When a decision has been made by a Referee, he shall announce it to the players.

Up to one hour before the commencement of a match either player may request a Referee or Marker other than appointed and this request may be considered and a substitute appointed. Players are not permitted to request any such change after the commencement of a match, unless both agree to do so. In either case the decision as to whether an official is to be replaced or not must remain in the hands of the Tournament Referee, where applicable.

23. DUTIES OF MARKER

(i)

The Marker calls the play and the score, with the server's score first. He shall call 'Fault', 'Foot-fault', 'Out' or 'Not up' as appropriate.

(ii)

If in the course of play, the Marker calls 'Not up' or 'Out', or 'Fault' or 'Foot-fault' to a second service, the rally shall cease.

(iii)

If the Marker's decision is reversed on appeal, a let shall be allowed, except as provided for in Rule 24 (ii) (d) and (e).

(iv)

Any service or return shall be considered good unless otherwise called.

(v)
After the server has served a fault, which has not been taken, the Marker shall repeat the score and add the words 'One Fault', before the server serves again. This call should be repeated should subsequent rallies end in a let, until the point is finally decided.

(vi)
When no Referee is appointed, the Marker shall exercise all the powers of a Referee.

(vii)
If the Marker is unsighted or uncertain, he shall call on the Referee to make the relevant decision; if the latter is unable to do so, a let shall be allowed.

24. DUTIES OF REFEREE

(i)
The Referee shall award Lets and Strokes and make decision: where called for by the rules, and shall decide all appeals, including those against the Marker's calls and decisions.

(ii)
He shall in no way intervene in the Marker's calling except:
(a) Upon appeal by one of the players;
(b) As provided for in Rule 17;
(c) When it is evident that the score has been incorrectly called, in which case he should draw the Marker's attention to the fact;
(d) When the Marker has failed to call the ball 'Not up' or 'Out', and on appeal he rules that such was in fact the case, the stroke should be awarded accordingly;
(e) When the Marker has called 'Not up' or 'Out', and on appeal he rules that this was not the case, a Let shall be allowed except that if in the Referee's opinion, the Marker's call had interrupted an undoubtedly winning return, he shall award the stroke accordingly;

(f) The Referee is responsible that all times laid down in the rules are strictly adhered to.

(iii)
In exceptional cases, the Referee may order:
(a) A player, who has left the court, to play on;
(b) A player to leave the court and to award the match to the opponent;
(c) A match to be awarded to a player whose opponent fails to be present in court within ten minutes of the advertised time of play;
(d) Play to be stopped in order to warn that the conduct of one or both players is leading to an infringement of the rules. A Referee should avail himself of this rule as early as possible when either player is showing a tendency to break the provisions of Rule 17;
(e) If after a warning a player continues to contravene Rule 20 (iii) then the Referee may award a game to the opponent.

25. COLOUR OF PLAYERS' CLOTHING

For amateur events under the control of the I.S.R.F. players are required to wear all white clothing. Member countries of the I.S.R.F. may legislate, if they so desire, to allow clothing of a light pastel colour to be worn for all other events under their control. (Note: Footwear is deemed clothing for this rule.) The Referee's decision thereon to be final.

APPENDIX I
Definitions

Board. The expression denoting a band, the top edge of which is 19 inches (.483m) from the floor across the lower part of the front wall above which the ball must be returned before the stroke is good.

Cut Line. A line set out upon the front wall, the top edge of which is six feet (1.829m) above the floor and extending the full width of the court. N.B. All lines in the court should be 2 inches (50mm) wide, and should be red.

Game Ball. The state of the game when the server requires one point to win is said to be 'Game Ball'.

Half-Court Line. A line set out upon the floor parallel to the side walls, dividing the back half of the court into two equal parts.

Hand-in. The player who serves.

Hand-out. The player who receives the service; also the expression used to indicate that hand-in has become hand-out.

Hand. The period from the time when a player becomes hand-in until he becomes hand-out.

Match Ball. The state of the match when the server requires one point to win is said to be Match Ball.

Not-up. The expression used to denote that a ball has not been served or returned above the board in accordance with the rules.

Out. The ball is out when it touches the front, sides or back of the court above the area prepared for play or passes over any cross bars or other part of the roof of the court. The lines delimiting such area, the lighting equipment and the roof are out of court.

Point. A point is won by the player who is hand-in and who wins a stroke.

Quarter-Court. One part of the back half of the court which has been divided into two equal parts by the half-court line.

Service Box or Box. A delimited area in each half court from within which hand-in serves.

Short Line. A line set out upon the floor parallel to and 18 feet (5.486m) from the front wall and extending the full width of the court.

Striker. The player whose turn it is to play after the ball has hit the front wall.

Stroke. A stroke is won by the player whose opponent fails to serve or make a good return in accordance with the rules.

Time or Stop. Expression used by the referee to stop play.

Tin. A strip of resonant material covering the lower part of the front wall between the Board and the floor.

Where to play

There are now many public sports centres throughout Britain where you can play without being a member. There is very often an admission charge to the centre and charges for the hire of courts vary due to the different periods of hire.

Listed below are the centres with more than four courts and some of the major squash clubs. The figure to the right of each denotes the number of courts within the centre.
* denotes sports centre

Avon
Bath*	4
Whitchurch*	4
Bristol LT	6
Lansdown, Bath	4

Bedfordshire
Bunyan, Bedford*	4
Dunstable*	6
Beadlow Manor, Shefford	4
Bedford County, Bedford	5
Knolls, Leighton Buzzard	6

Berkshire
Bracknell*	4
Maidenhead*	4
Montem, Slough*	5
East Berks, Maidenhead	7
Sindlesham	12

Buckinghamshire
Bletchley*	7
Wycombe*	6
Stantonbury, M. Keynes*	6
High Wycombe	5
Milton Keynes	7

Cambridgeshire
Kelsey Kerridge, Cambridge*	5
St Ives*	4
St Neots	6

Cheshire
Alsager School*	4
Bollington*	4
Leasowe*	4
Northgate, Chester*	4
Oval, Wirral*	6
Poynton*	4
Woolston, Warrington*	4
New Brighton RFC	6
Squash Runcorn	6
Stockport	8
West Cheshire, Chester	6

Cleveland
Eston, Middlesborough*	4
Stockton, YMCA*	4

Cornwall
Carn Brea, Redruth*	4
Polkyth, St Austell*	4

Cumbria
Whitehaven*	4
Carlisle	6

Derbyshire
Derby*	4
North Derbys, Chesterfield	7
South Derbys, Derby	6

Devon
Exeter University*	6
North Devon, Barnstaple*	4
Exeter Golf and Country	6

Dorset
Ferndown, Wimborne*	4
Poole*	4
West Hants, Bournemouth	4

Durham
Consett*	4
Newton Aycliffe*	4
Durham	7
Sunderland	6

Essex
Bramston (Witham)*	4
Epping*	4
Harlow*	10
Waltham Abbey*	4
Waterside Farm, Canvey I.*	4
Brenfield, Brentwood	10
Kingswood	12
Westcliff	9

Gloucestershire
Gloucester*	7
Stratford Park, Stroud*	4
Cheltenham	5
Gloucester	6

Hampshire
Alton*	6
Andover*	4
Applemore, Southampton*	4

Basingstoke* 4
Farnborough* 4
Fleet* 5
Fleming Park, Eastleigh* 5
Portsmouth 6
Winchester LT 6

Hertfordshire
Dacorum, Hemel Hempstead* 4
Hitchin* 4
Nicholas Hawksmoor,
  Borehamwood* 4
Stevenage* 7
Welwyn-Hatfield* 6
Woodside, Watford* 6
Potters Bar 6
St Albans 6

Kent
Northfleet* 6
Stour, Ashford* 4
White Oak, Dartford* 4
Medway 6
Rodmersham, Sittingbourne 6
Squash Welling 4
Whitstable 4

Lancashire
Castle, Bury* 4
Fulwood, Preston* 4
Hindley, Wigan* 4
Horwich, Bolton* 4
Hyndburn, Accrington* 4
William Thompson, Burnley* 4
Maple, Odham 6
Northern, Manchester 6
Park Hall, Chorley 6
West Lancs, Southport 6
Willows, Salford 6

Leicestershire
Hinckley* 6
Leicester New Parks 6
Squash Leicester 6
Wanlip Park CC, Syston 6

Lincolnshire
Grimsby* 4
Grantham 5

London
Crystal Palace* 10
Picketts Lock, Enfield* 8
Harrow* 12
Michael Sobell, Islington* 6
Crofton, Lewisham* 4
Redbridge* 4
Wanstead* 4
Westcroft, Sutton* 6
Beckenham CC 4
Bromley Sports 8
Connaught, Chingford 4

Coolhurst, N8 4
Coulsdon Court 6
Ealing 6
Lambton, W11 6
New Croydon 10
North Kensington 6
North Kent, Blackheath 6
North London, N10 6
South Kensington SW10 6
Wanstead 8
Wembley 15

Middlesex
North Middx, Enfield 8
Taywood, Northolt 6

Northumberland
Concordia, Cramlington* 6
Eldon Square, Newcastle* 7
Newbiggin* 4
Gateshead 6

Nottinghamshire
Bingham* 4
Nottingham 6
Plains, Mapperley 6
Trent Bridge 4
Carlton, Nottingham* 4
Grove, Newark* 4

Oxfordshire
Spiceball Park, Banbury* 4
Highfield, Oxford 8

Shropshire
Bridgnorth* 4
Oswestry* 4
Stirchley, Telford* 4
Shifnal 7

Somerset
Wellington* 4
Street 4

Staffordshire
Riverside, Stafford* 4
Gordon Country Club, Stoke 4
Wolverhampton 6

Surrey
Guildford* 4
Leatherhead* 6
Woking* 7
Mid Surrey, Ewell 8
West Surrey, Walton 7
Wimbledon 8

Sussex
Portslade* 4
Crawley* 4
Worthing* 5
Chichester 5
Haywards Heath 5
Mid-Sussex, Horsham 5

Warwickshire

Ken Marriott, Rugby* 4

West Midlands
Dudley* 6
Wyndley, Sutton Coldfield* 6
Birmingham 5
Brandon Hamm, Coventry 6
Coventry and N. Warwicks 6
Edgbaston Priory 8
North Birmingham 8
Nova, Coventry 6
Rugby Stag* 6

Wiltshire
Pleasure Dome, Swindon* 4

Books

The Story of Squash
Rex Bellamy, Cassell, £2.95.
Rex Bellamy is the lawn tennis
and squash correspondent of
The Times. There is no more
lucid commentator on the
game and no more enthusiastic
player. In this history, Bellamy
traces the game from its roots
and indulges in a little
intelligent guesswork where
only clues to the truth exist.
He introduces all the squash-
playing countries through the
stars they have produced. By
the end the reader will feel he
knows them as intimate
friends, such is Bellamy's
knowledge of the game's
personalities. The hard-ball
version is not ignored and
there are plenty of charming
anecdotes. All delightfully
written and heartily
recommended.

Geoff Hunt on Squash

Geoff Hunt and Alan Trengove, Cassell, £2.50.

This book by the current world champion assumes that the reader is at least familiar with the basics of the game. However it goes back to basic principles in order to check that nothing radical is going wrong. At least half the book is devoted to match play, attitudes, practice and fitness, with a particularly good question-and-answer section outlining Hunt's approach to the game. Clearly there is no better authority on how to play the attacking game, unless, of course, you prefer Jonah Barrington.

The Book of Jonah

Jonah Barrington and Clive Everton, Stanley Paul, £1.85.

This book, published in 1972, the last year Barrington won the British Open, traces Barrington's early life from childhood, through school and university, and gives the reader an insight into some of the factors which made Barrington turn to squash. Although there is no allusion to Barrington's 1964 Cornish county victory, which gives some indication of the standard he attained before he turned his entire attention to squash, the fact is that Barrington's story is quite remarkable. The years of success are detailed from the champion's own viewpoint and are interspersed with moments of anguish. A thoroughly interesting study of squash's greatest personality.

Barrington on Squash

Jonah Barrington, Stanley Paul, £2.75.

This instructive work deals briefly but succinctly with all the fundamentals of the game. What makes it different from other books on instruction is the feature which runs throughout the book entitled *Barrington's battles*.

Teach Yourself Squash Rackets

Leslie Hamer and Rex Bellamy, English Universities Press, 75p. Leslie Hamer devoted almost his entire life to the playing and teaching of squash. The professional at Mayfair's Bath Club for many years, he conducted many coaching courses for the SRA. No one is better qualified to give technical advice and the Bellamy prose enlivens a studious work.

Play Better Squash

John Beddington, Queen Anne Press, £3.95.

This slim instructional paperback was written when most of the world's leading players used the author's club as a practice home. He is therefore familiar with all the top players. But this book is for the beginner. The use of clear and effective diagrams leaves the reader in no doubt at all about the author's meaning.

World of Squash

Edited by Mike Palmer, Queen Anne Press, £3.95.

One of a series of excellent yearbooks by Queen Anne Press. In fact this is only the second of the squash yearbooks and it deals primarily with the events of the previous season. It contains reports from New Zealand, Australia and Europe, as well as articles on the game's leading personalities. Biographies of the players are a feature of these yearbooks as are the many fine action shots. It combines a good read with much information and could become a prime reference work.

SRA Handbook

Squash Rackets Association. Vast amounts of information are available in this handbook, published each year, together with plenty of comment on the events of the previous year as well. There is an impressive records section which includes all the major league results as well as the county open and closed tournament champions.

Magazines

The Squash Player

33 West Street, Brighton BN1 2KE.

The oldest established squash magazine, it is published monthly and contains reports and articles on current topics.

Squash Monthly

17 Farringdon St, London EC4. The second of the glossy monthlies, it covers similar ground and includes special sections on clubs and the trade.

Club Squash

Offices 1 & 2, Third Floor, National Liberal Club, Whitehall Place, London SW1. *Club Squash* began life as a give-away twice-monthly newspaper but is now a monthly. The newspaper format means that there are plenty of topics, making it a thoroughly good read.

Squash associations

Records

SQUASH ASSOCIATIONS

Squash Rackets Association
70 Brompton Road,
London SW3 1DX.

The Scottish SRA
8 Frederick Street,
Edinburgh.

The Welsh SRA
82 Heathway Heath,
Cardiff,
South Glamorgan.

The Irish SRA
5 Shrewsbury Lawn Extn.,
Cabinteely,
Co. Dublin.

Womens Squash Rackets Association
345 Upper Richmond Road,
West Sheen,
London SW14 8QN.

The Squash Rackets Professionals Association
127 Old Bath Road,
Cheltenham, Gloucs.

Veteran Squash Rackets Club
270 Chessington Road,
Ewell, Epsom,
Surrey.

THE OPEN CHAMPION-SHIP

1930	C. R. Read (Queen's Club)
*1930	D. G. Butcher (Conservative)
*1931	D. G. Butcher (Conservative)
*1932	F. D. Amr Bey
*1934	F. D. Amr Bey
*1935	F. D. Amr Bey
*1936	F. D. Amr Bey
*1937	F. D. Amr Bey
*1938	J. P. Dear (Prince's)
*1946	M. A. Karim (Gezira S.C.)
*1947	M. A. Karim (Gezira S.C.)
1948	M. A. Karim (Gezira S.C.)
1949	M. A. Karim (Gezira S.C.)
1950	Hashim Khan (R.P.A.F. Peshawar)
1951	Hashim Khan (R.P.A.F. Peshawar)
1952	Hashim Khan (R.P.A.F. Risalpur)
1953	Hashim Khan (R.P.A.F. Risalpur)
1954	Hashim Khan (R.P.A.F. Risalpur)
1955	Hashim Khan (R.P.A.F. Risalpur)
1956	Roshan Khan (R.P.N. Karachi)
1957	Hashim Khan (Pakistan Air Force)
1958	Azam Khan (New Grampians S.R.C.)
1959	Azam Khan (New Grampians S.R.C.)
1960	Azam Khan (New Grampians S.R.C.)
1961	Azam Khan (New Grampians S.R.C.)
1962	Mohibullah Khan (Pakistan)
1963	A. Aboutaleb (U.A.R.)
1964	A. Aboutaleb (U.A.R.)
1965	A. Aboutaleb (U.A.R.)
1966	J. P. Barrington (Ireland)
1967	J. P. Barrington (Ireland)
1968	G. B. Hunt (Australia)
1969	J. P. Barrington (Ireland)
1970	J. P. Barrington (Ireland)
1971	J. P. Barrington (Ireland)
1972	J. P. Barrington (Ireland)
1973	G. B. Hunt (Australia)
1974	Q. Zaman (Pakistan)
1975	G. B. Hunt (Australia)
1976	G. B. Hunt (Australia)
1977	G. B. Hunt (Australia)
1978	G. B. Hunt (Australia)

*From its institution until 1947 the championship was played on the challenge system, with home and home matches and the stipulation that a third match should be played if the results of the first two were level.

OPEN PLATE COMPETITION

1968	D. Broom (S. Africa)
1969	T. C. Francis
1970	S. Muneer (Pakistan)
1971	A. Nadi (Egypt)
1972	B. Patterson
1973	A. A. Aziz (Egypt)
1974	A. A. Aziz (Egypt)
1975	M. Helal (Egypt)
1976	M. Helal (Egypt)
1977	D. Williams (Australia)

OPEN VETERANS' CHAMPIONSHIP

1964	A. A. T. Seymour-Haydon
1965	Nazrullah Khan
1966	Nazrullah Khan

1967	Nazrullah Khan
1968	Jamal Din
1969	Nazrullah Khan
1970	Jamal Din
1971	Jamal Din
1972	Jamal Din
1973	Jamal Din
1974	M. Buck
1975	M. Buck
1976	K. E. Parker
1977	K. E. Parker

OPEN VINTAGE CHAMPIONSHIP

1975	Jamal Din
1976	Jamal Din
1977	Hashim Khan

THE AMATEUR CHAMPIONSHIP

1922	T. O. Jameson
1923	T. O. Jameson
1924	W. D. Macpherson
1925	V. A. Cazalet
1926	J. E. Tomkinson
1927	V. A. Cazalet
1928	W. D. Macpherson
1929	V. A. Cazalet
1930	V. A. Cazalet
1931	F. D. Amr Bey
1932	F. D. Amr Bey
1933	F. D. Amr Bey
1934	C. P. Hamilton
1935	F. D. Amr Bey
1936	F. D. Amr Bey
1937	F. D. Amr Bey
1938	K. C. Gandar-Dower
1939	
to	No competition
1945	
1946	N. F. Borrett
1947	N. F. Borrett
1948	N. F. Borrett
1949	N. F. Borrett
1950	N. F. Borrett
1951	G. Hildick-Smith (S. Africa)
1952	A. Fairbairn
1953	A. Fairbairn
1954	R. B. R. Wilson
1955	I. Amin (Egypt)
1956	R. B. R. Wilson
1957	N. H. R. A. Broomfield
1958	N. H. R. A. Broomfield
1959	I. Amin (Egypt)
1960	M. A. Oddy

1961	M. A. Oddy
1962	K. Hiscoe (Australia)
1963	A. A. Jawaid (Pakistan)
1964	A. A. Jawaid (Pakistan)
1965	A. A. Jawaid (Pakistan)
1966	J. P. Barrington
1967	J. P. Barrington
1968	J. P. Barrington
1969	G. B. Hunt (Australia)
1970	G. Alauddin (Pakistan)
1971	G. Alauddin (Pakistan)
1972	C. Nancarrow (Australia)
1973	Mohibullah Khan (Pakistan)
1974	Mohibullah Khan (Pakistan)
1975	K. H. Shawcross (Australia)
1976	B. Brownlee (New Zealand)
1977	G. Awad (Egypt)
1978	G. Awad (Egypt)

AMATEUR CHAMPIONSHIP PLATE COMPETITION

1949	W. R. Howson
1950	A. P. Pellew
1951	C. N. Campbell
1952	M. T. Turnbull
1953	S. Lam
1954	H. de B. Priestly
1955	A. W. H. Mallett
1956	J. C. Gordon
1957	J. C. Gordon
1958	J. C. Gordon
1959	R. D. Montgomerie
1960	M. W. Corby
1961	E. R. Brotherton (S. Africa)
1962	M. J. Maisels (S. Africa)
1963	J. G. A. Lyon
1964	J. D. Ward
1965	N. J. Faulks
1966	D. B. Hughes
1967	D. M. Innes
1968	R. Zacks (Rhodesia)
1969	N. J. Faulks
1970	D. M. Innes
1971	P. G. Kirton
1972	P. G. Kirton
1973	P. G. Kirton
1974	A. R. H. Colburn (S. Africa)

1975	F. Donnelly (Australia)
1976	N. Ingledew (S. Africa)
1977	N. Ingledew (S. Africa)

THE AMATEUR VETERANS' CHAMPIONSHIP

1951	G. O. M. Jameson
1952	G. O. M. Jameson
1953	G. O. M. Jameson
1954	G. O. M. Jameson
1955	G. O. M. Jameson
1956	H. W. P. Whiteley (S. Africa)
1957	F. R. D. Corbett
1958	F. R. D. Corbett
1959	F. R. D. Corbett
1960	F. R. D. Corbett
1961	B. C. Phillips
1962	A. A. T. Seymour-Haydon
1963	A. A. T. Seymour-Haydon
1964	A. A. T. Seymour-Haydon
1965	R. S. Bourne
1966	R. S. Bourne
1967	R. B. R. Wilson
1968	R. B. Hawkey
1969	R. B. Hawkey
1970	R. B. Hawkey
1971	R. B. Hawkey
1972	W. D. N. Vaughan
1973	R. B. Hawkey
1974	R. B. Hawkey
1975	N. Lieberman (S. Africa)
1976	J. Platts
1977	J. Platts

THE AMATEUR VINTAGE CHAMPIONSHIP

1976	R. S. Bourne
1977	J. W. Dengel

BRITISH AMATEUR (CLOSED)

1974	J. C. A. Leslie
1975	P. N. Ayton
1976	J. C. A. Leslie
1977	P. S. Kenyon

BRITISH UNDER-23 CHAMPIONSHIP

1975	P. S. Kenyon
1976	G. Briars
1977	G. Briars

Glossary of terms

Ace: a service which is so good that the receiver is unable to return it.

Angle: a shot played to the nearest side wall from the front of the court in an attacking manner, so that the ball 'dies' into the opposite side wall.

Appeal: a player can appeal against some marking decisions or appeal for a let to the referee.

Backhand: any shot which comes to the left-hand side of a right-handed player as he faces the front wall.

Backswing: the portion of the stroke where the racket is taken back behind the body in preparation for the strike.

Back-wall boast: *in extremis* the only way to keep the ball going in a rally is to play the ball directly onto the back wall first before rebounding onto the front wall.

Board: the small strip of wood above the tin which marks the lower out-of-court limit on the front wall.

Boast: defensive shot, played from the back corners in the same way as the angle. Should only be played when there is no alternative as it is easily anticipated.

Clinger: down-the-wall shot which 'clings' to the side wall throughout its return from the front wall.

Crowding: when a player is in a position which denies an opponent a free swing at the ball, he is guilty of crowding and may have a penalty point awarded against him.

Cut: a spin, similar to slice, in which the racket comes under the ball, causing it to fall sharply after it hits the front wall. Often used in the drop shot and kill.

Cut line: the middle of the three lines on the front wall which determines whether or not the service is a fault.

Double boast: an imperfect boast in which the ball, instead of hitting side wall, front wall, side wall, in that order, hits side wall, side wall, front wall.

Down: expression to indicate that the ball hit the board or below.

Downswing: the portion of the swing from preparation until impact.

Drop shot: a short shot which hits the front wall just above the board and bounces on the floor very close to the front wall.

Fair view: each player must give his opponent an adequate sighting of the ball, after it has been played.

Fault: a foul service.

Follow-through: the portion of the swing after impact.

Forehand: any shot which comes to the right-hand side of a right-handed player as he faces the front wall.

Freedom to play: each player must allow his opponent room to strike the ball freely (see also Crowding).

Gallery: space above the court where spectators are able to watch.

Game: a game consists of the first player to reach nine points with a two-point margin in his favour. At eight-points-all, the receiver has the option of 'no set' or 'set 2' (see below).

Game ball: marking term used when 'hand in' stands within one point of game.

Half-court line: the line running at right angles to the front wall in the rear half of the court.

Half-volley: an improvised shot played immediately after the bounce.

Hand: the period during which a player holds the service, e.g. 'he went from 4—0 to 8—0 in one hand'

Hand in: the server.

Hand out: the receiver.

Interference: where a player denies an opponent fair view or freedom to play the ball.

Kill: a hard hit, cut shot, which dies close to the front wall.

Knock-up: preparation or practice time of five minutes

before commencing a match.

Length: a ball which hits the rear wall after bouncing once on the floor but before bouncing twice, and with such pace that it remains close to the back wall.

Let: a replayed point.

Lob: a shot which rises after hitting the front wall so that it clears the opponent's head and lands in the back of the court as near as possible to the back wall.

Marker: official who scores and decides all issues of fact, e.g. whether or not the service was a fault.

Masking: technique where a player in the forecourt hides the direction he intends to play the ball by covering the ball with his body. (Note: the player must immediately retreat from his opponent's line of vision. If he does not, he will have denied fair view.)

Nick: shot which hits the wall and the floor simultaneously so that the ball rolls along the floor as it rebounds.

No set: a receiver may elect to play just one point to decide who wins a game when the score has reached eight-all (see also Sudden death).

Not up: term used to indicate that the ball has bounced twice on the floor.

Opening up the court: playing a shot to manoeuvre an opponent out of position so that the next shot will be a winner into the large gap created.

Out of court: a ball which

hits the walls above the uppermost lines which surround the court.

Penalty point: a free point may be awarded to a player whose opponent has denied him fair view and/or freedom to play the ball.

Play: expression used by the marker (now infrequently used) to indicate to the players that a doubtful ball was good in his opinion.

Put out: term to describe a server who has lost the preceding rally and who has thus become 'hand out'.

Rally: sequence of good alternate shots which is ended by a winner, a loser, intervention by the referee or an appeal by either player.

Receiver: 'hand out'.

Referee: an additional official to the marker who decides all appeals by the players and who may intervene without an appeal to award a let or a penalty point.

Service: the shot which begins all rallies or points.

Service box: the squares behind the short line from which the server must deliver his service.

Set 2: a receiver may elect to play 2 points to decide the game when the score has reached eight-points-all.

Short line: the line which runs parallel to the front wall.

Skid boast: a variety of boast used only by advanced players, which rises rapidly from the side wall onto the front wall, so

that it comes back something like a lob.

Slice: a spin caused by the racket face coming across and slightly under the ball.

Smash: a variation of volley, similar to the smash in tennis, when the ball is played directly above the head.

Striker: the player whose turn it is to play the ball next.

Sudden death: a term used to describe the situation when a receiver elects no set at eight-points-all.

T: the junction of the short and half court lines which is the landmark which dominates the game.

Ten seconds: call made by the marker to warn both players that they have ten seconds in which to return to court to play the next game.

Time: expression used by the marker or referee when asking players to cease play, or at the end of the one-minute interval allowed during games.

Tin: the area below the board.

Turning: describes a player following the ball round the side and back walls in order to play the ball. (Note: this kind of stroke should be avoided as it is dangerous and likely to cause injury.)

Up: expression generally used in disputes to indicate that the ball was above the board or tin on the front wall, or that the ball was played before the second bounce.

Volley: a stroke played before the ball has bounced.

Index

Credits

Artists
Sally Launder
David Worth

Photographs
Colorsport, 19, 78
Robin Ely Jones, 22, 23

Mary Evans Picture Library,
   6, 7
Steve Powell, 4–5, 14, 17,
   24–5, 26, 30, 32–3, 34, 35,
   38, 39, 40–41, 42, 43, 44–5,
   47, 51, 53, 54, 59, 60–61,
   62
Steve Powell/Allsport, 11, 20,
   46, 67, 68–9, 72, 76, 77
Sport and General, 10, 70, 71,
   73, 78
Women's Squash Rackets
   Association, 79

If copyright in any photograph
reproduced in this publication
has been unwittingly infringed,
the publishers tender their
apologies and will be glad of
the opportunity, upon being
satisfied as to the owner's
title, to pay an appropriate fee.

Cover
Design: Barry Kemp
Photograph: Steve Powell/
   Allsport